New Voices

7th Issue
Fall 1996 - Spring 1997

Developmental Writing Program
Department of English

California State University, Northridge

*The diversity of our student population provides a variety of life experiences,
and we are enriched by the insights shared by men and women,
natives and immigrants, and youthful and mature writers.*

*Louanne Kennedy, Provost and Vice President for Academic Affairs,
California State University, Northridge*

Sandra Jackson, Editor
Instructor, Department of English

Pamela Bourgeois, Coordinator
Developmental Writing Program
Department of English

Colleen D. Schaeffer, Technical Editor
Instructor, Department of English

KENDALL/HUNT PUBLISHING COMPANY
4050 Westmark Drive   Dubuque, Iowa 52002

Copyright © 1996, 1997 by Pamela Bourgeois

Library of Congress Catalog Number: 97-074143

ISBN 0-7872-4203-9

All rights reserved. No part of this publication may be reproduced,
stored in a retrieval system, or transmitted, in any form or by any
means, electronic, mechanical, photocopying, recording, or otherwise,
without the prior written permission of the copyright owner.

Printed in the United States of America
10 9 8 7 6 5 4 3 2 1

Preface

Welcome to our seventh issue of *New Voices*, a publication of work from the students in the Developmental Writing Program at California State University, Northridge. For the past three and a half years, CSUN students have been taking their English classes, indeed all of their Humanities classes, in Zelzah Court, a dusty oasis on the North Campus temporarily established after the 1994 earthquake which devastated the campus.

The good news is that we are returning to Jerome Richfield Hall (formerly Sierra North) and Sierra Tower for the Fall, 1997 semester. Students and faculty will be meeting and conferencing in newly rebuilt, refurbished, and re-furnished classrooms and offices. As the movers were packing my books and files and assorted paraphernalia gathered during these last three years, I thought of our developing writing students who had never seen our normally beautiful campus building on the quad adjacent to the stately Oviatt Library, or strolled between classes across the lawns to the Matador Bookstore complex. Instead they had visited these sites via different, more difficult routes along construction sites. I thought of their pleasure when they would be sitting in classrooms with solid walls and ceilings, computer monitors, and VCRs, and windows overlooking the reassuring presence of other campus buildings glimpsed through leafy shade trees.

The rebuilding of the central campus was not the only reconstruction going on this year. Writing Faculty from the departments of English, Chicano Studies, and Pan African Studies gathered to address, refine, and make workable the outcomes and objectives for our Developmental Writing Program that the writing coordinators had worked on last summer. The faculty met for several Saturday workshops examining syllabi in light of these outcomes and objectives, discussing classroom strategies and campus resources, and considering assessment models.

This year our developmental writing students benefited from this examination and refocusing effort. The *New Voices* Editorial Board and the judges were impressed with the quality of student writing we were seeing in the submissions (over 250). We found it a pleasant chore to have so many well-written, interesting essays to choose from in making the difficult final selections for publication.

As I was walking back to my office in Building 15 from Zelzah Court after my last final, I caught a glimpse of a truck from Physical Plant Management with the bumper sticker "NOT JUST BACK... BETTER!" on its rear bumper. This was the rallying cry President Blenda Wilson gave the campus to encourage the faculty, students and staff who were returning to the devastation of three and a half years ago. And I knew in a flash of hope and insight that this statement on a bumper sticker really applies to our developmental writing students who are sturdily and determinedly writing their way into academic literacy. They too will be back next year, and not only back, but better able to express themselves in their own new voices.

Pamela Bourgeois, Coordinator
June 26, 1997
Northridge, California

Acknowledgments

A good essay must draw its curtain around us,
but it must be a curtain that shuts us in, not out.
Virginia Woolf

To those students whose essays are published in *New Voices '97,* thank you for sharing your lives and ideas with us—thank you for allowing us a glimpse behind your curtain.

Once again, it has been a delight to work with Pamela Bourgeois, who keeps the Developmental Writing Program operating so smoothly. Thanks for your energetic encouragement, Pam, as well as all the scrumptious sandwiches! To Colleen Schaeffer, our technical editor, thanks for your efficiency, your cooperation, and your patience when I phone you at all hours.

The Developmental Writing Faculty continues to be highly supportive of this publication and we appreciate this so much. Our marvelous Editorial Board rallied around *New Voices* once again, to read and select from the 252 submissions. We could not do it without you! The Board members are: Debby Bogard, Edna Burow, Eve Caram, Fran Grimes, Kara Klima, Anne Kellenberger, Sharon Maselli, Amy Reynolds, Lynne Rosenberg, Marilyn Segal, Sharon Smartt, Pat Swenson, Nancy Taylor, and Mary Beth Tegan.

Special thanks must go to this year's judges: William Walsh, outgoing Chair of the English Department; Joanna McKenzie, Educational Coordinator, College of Extended Learning; and Patrick Hunter, coordinating judge and Instructor in the Department of English. We thank you for your support, your time, and your expertise.

To Robert Noreen, incoming Chair of the Department of English, thank you for your continued encouragement and assistance. To Bradley Peters, our new Director of Composition, we appreciate your warm endorsement of this publication. To Pat Murray, Barbara Kroll, and Evelyn McClave, thanks for being there!

We are grateful to Jorge Garcia, Dean of the School of Humanities, and Margaret Fieweger, Associate Vice President of Academic Programs, for helping to maintain this publication through the years.

As always, Karin Castillo has been not only helpful, but innovative, and humorous as well. Thanks must also go to Nancy Thompson, Nancy Bernstein, and Jennifer Elliott for their efficiency and assistance.

Thank you to the Northridge Textbook Exchange (NTX) for sponsoring our prizes once more.

To my family, (my husband, Ces, and children, Katie and David), thanks for everything. You're the best!

Finally, to all the students in the Developmental Writing Program, thank you for responding to this publication with such zest. In the words of one of our students: *"New Voices* is a way of getting a totally honest reaction or opinion from new students about life as they see it. All the essays that I read had a different effect on me. Some made me sad, some made me laugh, but all of them made me feel something, all the essays did succeed in making me think" (Jason Francisco, English 098, Spring 1997).

To all those who have played a part in the publication of *New Voices* this year, it has been a privilege and a pleasure to work with you.

Sandra Jackson
Northridge, California
June, 1997

iv

New Voices '97 Writing Awards

The following students will receive cash prizes or NTX book vouchers at an
awards ceremony in Fall '97:

Narrative Essays:
1st Place: Kate Beylin, *Laundry Exchange*
2nd Place: Yuria Takehana, *An Apparition*
Honorable Mention: Sergio Miramontes, *El Coyote*

Text-Based Essays:
1st Place: Mary Barmakian, *Water Or Chocolate*
2nd Place: Jason Spadaro, *"The Open Boat": A Symbol for Life*
Honorable Mention: Thuc Duy Phan, *The Impermanence of Life*
Cindy Hemmings, *A Moral Lesson*
Reena Parmar, *M. Butterfly*

Persuasive Essays:
1st Place: Tu Minh Tran, *Public Television*
2nd Place: Cedrick Holmes, *If You Don't Live Where I Live, You Can't See What I See*
Honorable Mention: Javier Pina, *Is the DARE Program Effective at the Elementary
Level?*

Creative/Journal Entries:
Special Creative Award: Colleen Devlin, *The Mission of a Lifetime*
Special Creative Award: Rima Ballout, *The Godfather*

Judges:
Patrick Hunter, Coordinating Judge; Instructor, Department of English
Joanna McKenzie, Educational Coordinator, College of Extended Learning
William Walsh, Chair, Department of English

New Voices '97 **Editorial Board:**
Debby Bogard
Pamela Bourgeois (Coordinator, Developmental Writing Program)
Edna Burow
Eve Caram
Fran Grimes (Former Co-Editor)
Sandra Jackson (Editor)
Kara Klima
Anne Kellenberger
Sharon Maselli

Amy Reynolds
Lynne Rosenberg (Former Editor)
Colleen Schaeffer (Technical Editor)
Marilyn Segal
Sharon Smartt
Pat Swenson
Nancy Taylor
Mary Beth Tegan

Photographs:
Sandra Jackson
Anne Kellenberger
Lynne Rosenberg

Original Art Work:
Cover and Drawing on page 31: Cesar Guevara, English 097, Fall 1996

Developmental Writing Faculty

Table of Contents

"What is reading but silent conversation?"

— Walter Savage Landor, "Aristoteles and Callisthenes," *Imaginary Conversations* (1824-53)

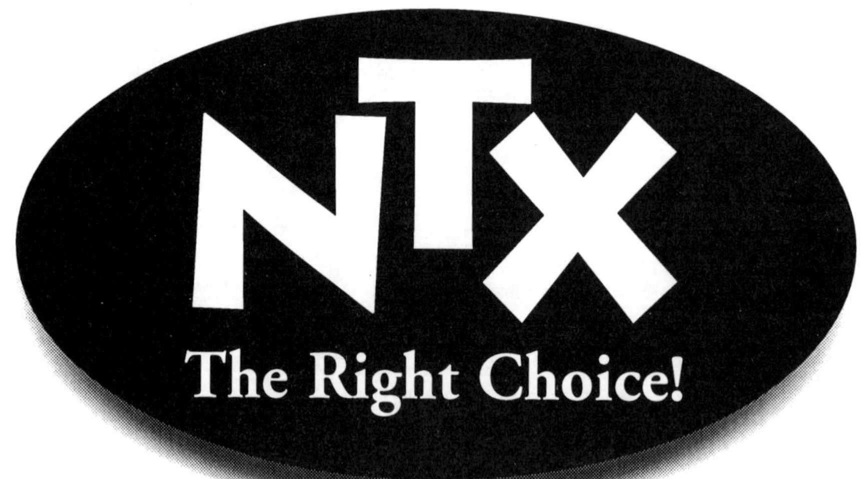

Proud sponsor
of the 1997 edition of

New Voices

At CSUN you have a choice in bookstores.
Those who know choose

Narrative
Essays

New Voices '96 Awards Ceremony

A word is a bud, attempting to become a twig.
Gaston Bachelard

Kate Beylin--1st Place Narrative Essay
English 097
Instructor: Anne Kellenberger

Laundry Exchange

It all began on a Sunday afternoon at the Laundromat. I had been in New York for the holidays visiting my grandfather who lives in Queens. Living in California, I had forgotten how cold it gets during this time of year. And although I had spent a great deal of my time complaining about the freezing weather, I think deep down inside I was excited to witness the first signs of a potentially white Christmas. As I stared outside the tall, transparent windows of the Laundromat at the usual crowd of people occupying the busy streets of New York, I realized how much I had missed the racy, exciting atmosphere of the city that never sleeps.

My grandfather had talked me into doing the laundry, my least favorite thing in the world to do, but how could I refuse? If only he knew some of the results from my previous attempts to wash my garments, he probably would not have asked me to take care of his. Nevertheless, there I was, reading the directions printed on the back of the detergent box, cursing at the inconsistent directions. I know for a fact that laundry cannot be done in three simple steps! There wasn't even a clear explanation on how to properly divide the colors. Sure, it says darks together, lights together, but the label clearly discriminates against dark polkadots on a light background or vivid colored stripes, and what am I supposed to do if the fabrics are different? Frustrated, I shoved everything into one machine, dropped in the required amount of change and sat down to wait for the ordeal to be over. To help kill some time, I picked up a magazine and began flipping through the pages. After a while, I looked up and noticed that some bum off the street had entered the Laundromat and was harassing some of the other people doing their laundry. I kept thinking to myself that it's all about eye contact; if you don't make eye contact they won't approach you. But I couldn't help but stare at him. He was a rather old, white man draped in layers of soiled clothes. Basically he looked like the typical "guy off the street." I continued to observe him.

Although I was not at a distance where I could hear what this man was saying, I could read his body language. His gestures were quick and large; he almost looked like he was preparing himself to fly. I wanted to know what he was so passionate about. I leaned forward so I could hear what he was saying to the other man next to him, but still I was unable to make out his sentences. The other man reached into his pockets and pulled out some change and extended it to the bum. What I saw next really surprised me. The bum wouldn't accept the money; instead he kept asking the man for something else. I couldn't help but wonder what he was asking him for. Did he want more money? A cigarette? "No way mister. Get lost. I don't have time for that." The man spat as he turned away from the bum and continued with his laundry business. The more I watched this scenario the more compelled I became. I wanted to know what this man wanted, if he didn't want money. He went up to several other people and confronted them, but the responses were all the same. No one seemed to want to hear him or waste another moment of conversation with him. "Get away from me you crazy * * * * !" I jumped back, startled to hear that remark so casually thrown out. I had to remind myself this was New York--where nothing was too unusual!

Just as I was finishing my thought, I saw his eyes meet mine. Oh no! I had done what I had set out to avoid. I had made eye contact with him. It seemed like an eternity as our eyes met and held. He looked at me with such penetrating eyes that I began to feel naked, as if my entire soul was exposed and this strange man I had never seen before in my life knew all my anxieties and fears. His eyes were intimidating me to a point of physical discomfort that was almost painful. I began to feel my knees tremble. Quickly, I dropped my eyes and began frantically turning the pages of the magazine that was on my lap.

Did I know this man from somewhere? Was it possible that we had met before? Why was he affecting me so much? Could it be that I had inhaled too much of that fabric softener? I didn't want to look up because I was afraid our eyes would meet, but I found it impossible to control my curiosity. I decided to take a quick peek. However, the moment I looked up he began walking over in my direction. I decided it was definitely a bad move--I should not have peeked.

As he was walking towards me I kept thinking: "Well, at least now he'll satisfy my queries." I began to cross and uncross my legs, knocking down the soda next to my chair, but I didn't bother picking it up. I couldn't concentrate on anything else. Anxious to know what he was going to say to me, I began biting my lower lip. This is a normal reaction for me when I get nervous. He was moving so quickly before, why was everything suddenly in slow motion? I was beginning to get very irritated by the lack of...but before I could even finish my thought, the front entrance door abruptly swung open as two officers entered the Laundromat and headed directly for the bum. Someone must have made a call about him disturbing some of the people in the Laundromat. The two officers placed his hands behind his back and firmly held onto his shoulders as they began to escort him out.

As I continued to watch, I realized I was resenting the officers' interruption. Now I would never know what this desperate looking man wanted from everyone in the Laundromat. He didn't fight the officers; in fact he silently accepted his fate and allowed them to have their way with him. But as they walked by me, the man suddenly stopped. Once again he looked into my eyes. Only this time I didn't want to look away; oddly, I realized I wanted to help this man. But what could I do? For the first time in my life I felt extremely helpless; I had no control over the situation. I didn't even have control over my own emotions!

The officers urged him to continue walking, and he did, but right before they reached the exit he turned to me and mouthed "Will you pray for me?" I didn't respond. I simply didn't know what to say. "Will you pray for me?" he repeated, as I uncomfortably looked away. Within moments he was out of the Laundromat, but his presence lingered in my mind all day.

After reviewing the entire scenario I realized he wasn't asking anyone for money, he was asking for recognition. Recognition as a human being! Every person in that Laundromat was willing to give him spare change, but not a single person would say a prayer for him. A simple prayer extending a degree of compassion with faith--absolutely free of charge. Yet no one would do it. Has our society entered the realm of dehumanization? When did we achieve such confidence in ourselves that we took on this attitude of superiority and indifference? This man was just another man with problems like everyone else. Everyone has his or her own story. How can we collectively judge this individual who is not any less human than we are?

I am not a very religious person, but that night I prayed. I prayed for that man whom I shamelessly addressed as "the bum," and I prayed for the world. And I also prayed that I would never have to do the laundry again; it is much too stressful!

Chris Aghayan
English 098
Instructor: Debby Bogard

Tough Guy

As a young boy I was never a tough kid, a fighter. Though I possessed a devious mind, I played most of the games by the rules. Stereotypically speaking, you can never sound tough when you're the president of a chess club, but my father had a different view of this young Hercules. He saw the heart of a lion behind this sensitive creature, and the eyes of a tiger through these convex glasses.

By the time I reached puberty, my father had signed me up at a local boxing gym. It was one of the most horrifying experiences of my life. I was scheduled for a two-hour voluntary beating, three times a week. I'm not sure if my father's intentions were to help me grow up faster in my puberty days, or have my bones crushed while I was developing a bone structure. As time went by, I grew into liking this sport, then I decided to put more effort into it, to make the best of it. For some odd reason (maybe divine) the coach found a special interest in me. He said I had good reflexes and stamina and suggested that I should participate in a local amateur feather-weight boxing match.

The tournament day arrived and my feet were like cotton candy. I'm not sure what was holding me up. My mind took every event in the past nine months of my training and played it back in fast-forward, like a video machine. It all looked like the Sisyphean labor, and today was the day to watch the rock that I'd rolled up, roll down. I don't remember how I entered the ring. I was a floating pair of eyes, focusing as hard as I could to see through my sweat. I don't even remember my opponent's face. What I remember best is how red and painful those gloves looked; they were my enemy, not the person hiding behind them. I thought to myself, "If I can dodge those red bulldogs for a few rounds, I'll be all right."

The bell rang, and my heart exploded. I walked towards my execution post, steady and confident, then we started to exchange hatred; some of his jabs were stronger than mine...

The bell rang, and the final round began. Despite all the bruises and cuts I must have had, I felt very little pain. To me, this was the closest thing to laboring in a prison camp: no food, no rest and not much water. I was still standing, maybe to make my father happy, or maybe because I just hated my opponent so much. The cheering of the crowd roared like underwater voices, but made no sense. Every image was sharp, yet in one dimension; one of my eyes must have been shut. I was breathing like a galloping horse, tired and steady. My coach's voice kept echoing in my head, 'Guards up, guards up.' Numbness still hadn't taken over when the bell was hit with the hammer for the last time. The sound of that bell echoed in my head, like the sound of the Sunday church bell; it brought peace and conformity within me. This was the last ring I would have to endure. I had survived the execution--a miracle.

As the referee pulled my left arm, I followed him to the center of the ring, the spot that can make you a hero or hurt you harder than those punches you received in the past eight rounds.

My arm was so numb that I had to look to see whether he was going to raise it, or else I wouldn't have known if I had won or not. I took a slow glance at the referee. He turned to me, expressionless. I wasn't sure what it meant. Then I realized that the decision was out and my arm was still down. I was happy, very happy, because I wouldn't have to step into the ring again, and I was happy I had proved to my father that I wasn't that tough guy he thought I was.

Jenny Sargent
English 098
Instructor: Debby Bogard

My Own Little Field Trip

It was my first year on the quiet naval base in Pt. Mugu where my Dad, a petty officer in the Navy, had been transferred. I had just completed the first grade and summer was upon us. To substitute for my missed cousins, I was enrolled in Sunshine Summer Camp at the youth center. Living on the naval base (where security was utmost) and being the child of a mom who stressed self-reliance, I was allowed to make my own way to camp on my Princess Rose, a pink, banana-seated bike. I had been making this ride to the youth center for some weeks now. Every morning I awoke to six o'clock cartoons, greedily consumed two chocolaty bowls of Cocoa-puffs, and burst through the front door to the garage, minutes after my mom and younger brother had left for their own day. I don't ever remember seeing my Dad. Our morning good-byes were said with his tucking us in at night.

One morning I awoke again to the cool air, as I always had, but I sensed something different. My eyes darted to the clock; it would be some time before Papa Smurf, so why was I awake? Then every thought from the day before rushed back into my mind, sending me sprawling from my warm covers. Today was THE field trip, the field trip to Magic Mountain! I had to get ready! I had to find my sunshine-yellow camp bag--the one that had that peanut-butter and jelly smell and that we used for the trips to the beach and pool. After a frenzied hunt through my closet for the bag, the rest of my morning was a hasty blur of normal morning routines. Then, at last, it was time to leave.

I ran outside and grabbed the garage door handle. It was one of those old, wooden doors. I pulled at it and then pushed it up, but not quite all the way. It didn't matter. I had enough room to get my bike out and then I would be on my way to MAGIC MOUNTAIN. I rolled my bike out into the bumped-up tar driveway, set the kickstand and then ran to the black spring hinges from which the garage door extended. I was too small to really reach the string to pull the garage door down. I could sometimes reach it if I tried really hard and then used my weight to slowly bring it down. Today, though, I wasn't bored enough to try the two to four jumps it took to get the string. It was much easier to run over and yank on the springs and run out before the door crashed down. My parents must have witnessed this latter method one day, because I can remember them telling me not to "yank on the springs like that." I never cared enough to listen to them on this subject. They were parents. They didn't understand. I gave the springs a good jerk.

Before the darkness of the garage swallowed me, I saw the hinges clamp down on my fingers. Until my eyes could adjust, I could only feel the dull pain in my hands. I started screaming, and the tears came almost immediately. During this time, one hand came free and I could now see the other. The metal had already cut into the skin, and I just remember screaming "help!" in a voice that came from the back of my throat, and looking back and forth from my blurry hand to the blurry inside of the garage door. I couldn't understand why no one was helping me. I was screaming. Why wasn't anyone there? I got so angry and scared. I began to kick at the garage door and eventually it lifted enough, with one of the kicks, to loosen the clamp's metal grip on my fingers so that I could pull them free. I don't remember how I got out of the garage after that, but I remember watching the blood drip a little trail on the cement walkway and then the linoleum, as I went into the house. I was still crying and my fingers were throbbing, but I was better. I was no longer trapped. I got one of our green washcloths from the bathroom, wrapped it around my burning fingers, and went into the kitchen and called my mom at work. The line was busy, so I placed the phone, very calmly, back onto the hook and then bolted through the screen door to my bike. I was still crying. Why wasn't anyone there?

I pedaled in my own world of desperation to the youth center. I pedaled, wet with blood and tears, through those empty streets. The aching throb in my hand increased. My head echoed with the sound of my own heartbeat. I dropped my bike somewhere outside the youth center and stumbled into a sprint through the front door to find a counselor.

At first the building was empty, but then a counselor came from the office. I can only imagine what she thought when she found me standing there, holding my bloody, towel-wrapped hand up for her to see. I watched her mouth move, but I never heard the words she spoke. I just remember her tight hold as she led me into the bathroom by my good hand, to run water over my cuts and help me. I was where I needed to be. I had no more worries. I had someone to worry for me.

This was when I first learned that there's not always someone to get you out of trouble. You can never truly depend on anyone. Then, as a young child, I only knew this from feelings. As a young adult, I can now put those feelings into these words: "You have to help yourself first before anyone else can."

Everything was okay after I made it to the youth center. The counselors got hold of my mom and told her what had happened. She left work to pick me up and take me to the emergency room, where I received some stinging, piss-colored antiseptic to my index and middle fingers. Stitches, and some massive, white, gauze bandages were soon to follow. I was returned to the deserted youth center with a kiss and hug from my mom. The counselor who had washed my cuts out kept me entertained by wrapping her hand around my two fingers, fat with bandaging, and telling me they looked like Bugs Bunny popping his two ears out of his hole. She then proceeded to recite Elmer Fudd lines in between my exhausted giggles.

English 098
Instructor: Debby Bogard

1. a ghost
2. a sudden or unusual sight

An Apparition

Once I thought that my life was miserable. I was living with my sick grandma in a rustic agricultural village. When I was 12, I had to move to her house for some unknown reason. We were not happy with each other because I had hated her for a good while. She was an enemy of my family, and I found out the reason quite recently. She hated my mum who was her own daughter, and my mum hated her as much as she hated a frog. My mum said that Grandma was as noisy as a frog. Grandma was against my mum's marriage because my mum had run away from her first arranged marriage, which, of course, Grandma had organized.

Grandma's house was very old, with ghosts. My cousin said that she had seen a severed head of a Samurai, a Japanese warrior; my aunty was possessed by a dead soul while she was praying in front of the family Buddhist altar; my mum saw the light of a soul. I, myself, have seen something there. Actually, I have heard something, a noise of footsteps which resounded from the darkness in the quiet, old, wooden house.

Despite all the ghosts, I came to like the place very much, especially the back garden which led to the mountain behind. The mountain didn't belong to Grandma, but it seemed as if it did. Between the garden and the mountain there was a vegetable field, and Grandma and I took walks to see how the vegetables were growing. I liked the village, too. There was only one road which had just one lane. There was one fishmonger, a vegetable store and two general stores. I used to take my grandma to the stores, walking very slowly, hand in hand. I was surprised to see an imprint of Grandma's hand on my arm. She had to hold my arm so tightly to support herself. Step by step, I could feel her strength. I didn't know where her strength came from. My mum said that I had to push Grandma to keep walking, otherwise she would totally lose her ability to walk. I thought that as long as she had such strength, she would be fine, but I kept my word.

I tried to stay with Grandma as much as possible. But I had to go to school very early and come home late, so in order to spend some time with her, I studied in the living room with her loud TV noise at night. She would order a big box of peaches, oranges, grapes or apples (depending on the season) just for me. I had them after dinner, not because I loved fruits but because I needed to fill my stomach after our simple meal. She thought that I loved fruits. She wanted to do whatever she could do for me so that she could fulfill herself instead of feeling lonely.

"I'm not worth living," Grandma said one day. I asked why. She said that everybody hated her.

I think I laughed a bit and said to her, "What makes you think so, Grandma? I don't think so, anyway."

She was sure that everybody hated her because she had been very selfish to her husband, children, and the rest of the world. I knew that I was included. She said that her being left alone was punishment for this.

"I don't want to live any more. I want to die." She was wiping her eyes and nose with a tissue which had been in her pocket all day or longer.

"You are not alone, Grandma. You are with me, and we've got to help each other. You are worth living, at least to me."

Her fitful madness came back again and again. I consoled her each time, trying to tell her how much I needed her. We became close and started to depend on each other. Whenever she said that she wanted to die, I had to give her a reason that her life was worth living, which made me think about my own. I wasn't happy with my situation, away from my parents. I felt left alone. Whenever my mum called me, I said I was fine. Was I really?

One night, I woke up to the sound of footsteps moving very fluidly. They couldn't be Grandma's. She was afraid of walking. She would crawl if she needed to go to the toilet in the darkness. I heard the shoji, a sliding paper door, opening in Grandma's room, and then footsteps and the squeaking of the old wooden hallway. I didn't tell anybody about this, but I kept hearing the same sound every night. I thought that Grandma was lying to me, pretending that she couldn't walk. Who else could it be? Only the two of us were in that old house. So, if it wasn't me, it had to be her.

Eventually, I told my mum that something was funny, instead of "I'm fine." "I can hear the sound of footsteps every night. Can it be Grandma? They sound like very light steps, not like Grandma's usual steps."

After a few minutes of silence, my mum explained to me that Grandma's spirit-self walked every night, since she had a strong will to walk again. I interpreted to myself that being unable to walk made her want to die; however, she also had a strong will to live, otherwise she wouldn't wish to walk again. And I guessed that I was a part of the reason for her desire to live. She made her life worth living for me. And my life became worth living because Grandma needed me.

I didn't hear footsteps or squeaking any more after that. I still don't know whether the footsteps were made by Grandma's spirit-self or not. The sound of the footsteps might have been my imagination. But I believe that the footsteps were something more than just my imagination.

I was away from Grandma for the next five years; however, just before she lost herself in her death bed, she called my name. She said, according to my aunty who was nursing Grandma, "I bought some biscuits for Yuria. Where is she? Can you tell her that her biscuits are there when she comes back?" I was still something to her because she still cared for me. I remember her whenever I eat fruits, but they never taste as good as the fruits which Grandma bought for me.

Samira Kasam
English 098
Instructor: Fran Grimes

Trapped in the Culture Zone

I have no problem with acting Indian, or dressing Indian. I am proud of my culture and I am proud to admit that I am an Indian, but sometimes I think my parents just go too far. "You should never forget your culture and your traditions," my parents say. "So what if you live in America, you are still Indian. You have to be proud of being Indian. You have to dress Indian, talk Indian, eat Indian, and most of all, act Indian." I am not the only "Indian girl" who gets these monthly lectures from my parents. My friends go through the same thing. Being a first generation "American" is a challenge in terms of "Open Parental Communication." My parents happen to be very strict and extremely old fashioned which makes it very hard for me to communicate with them.

I am 18 years old and still living with my parents. "Why?" you ask. I'll tell you why. An Indian girl can't leave her parents' house until she is married. She can't have boyfriends, and she can't go out with any guy until she is engaged and, of course, after that the only guy she would be allowed to go out with would be her fiancee.

So now you might ask why my parents are so strict. Well, my parents are afraid that I might forget my culture and inherit the "American Culture." They are also afraid that I might start dating and either end up getting pregnant or end up marrying someone they don't approve of. My parents do a good job to avoid that from happening. I can't talk to boys or have them call me, and if they do end up calling me, I get questioned.

"Why did he call? What did he want?"

"He just wanted to know what our math homework was."

"How old is he?"

"Nineteen, Mom."

"What nationality?"

"He's Russian."

"How do you know him?"

"He sits next to me in my math class."

"What's his name?"

"Roman."

My parents hold a strong belief in arranged marriages and that is why they happen to be strict in some cases. My parents' marriage was arranged. My mom didn't even get to see my dad until the day before their engagement. My dad, on the other hand, had seen my mom's picture. My mom didn't have a choice to marry whoever she wanted to marry. She was forced to marry my dad. My parents weren't the only "arranged couple." The traditions of arranged marriages has been in India for generations. First it was my great grandparents, then my grandparents; it came down to my parents, and I happen to be the next victim.

"I will find the perfect man for you. A Doctor or an Engineer. I'll throw you a big wedding and buy you a new car as a wedding present," says my dad. All I want to say is "Dream on."

There is no way I am getting into an arranged marriage. I choose who I want to be with and with whom I want to spend my life. I mean, think about it. What if he's a bad kisser, or horrible in bed, or has a major attitude problem, is too controlling, too dumb, too stupid, has a weird laugh, a long nose, is too skinny, too fat, too dark, buck-toothed, etc., etc., etc.? See what I mean? The worst part about arranged marriages is that there is no return policy. If you don't like it you can't return it or exchange it for something better. At times I feel like taking a bucket full of water and dumping it over their heads and saying, "Wake up. You're in the 90's."

My friends always tell me, "Why don't you try talking to them? Maybe talking to them might straighten things out and, if not, at least it might bring you a little closer than before." All I have to say is, "Been there, done that." It goes in through one ear and out the other. It's just like talking to a wall. Everything you throw bounces back at you. I remember talking to my mom once about her problem with boys calling me. It wasn't really a good idea, and she was mad, really mad.

I asked her, "Mom why am I not allowed to talk to boys or have them call me?"

"Because, first you will start talking to him, then maybe start liking him and the next thing you know you will probably want to go out with him."

"I don't think so mom; after all, don't you trust me?"

"I do trust you. It's the boys I don't trust. They like taking advantage of girls. Don't you watch the news. There are 13-year-old girls getting pregnant."

"But mom I am not 13. I am 18. I can take care of myself."

"No you can't."

"But mom..."

"I don't want to hear anything else; that's it."

I came to discover that talking to my mom about boys wouldn't do anything but hurt her feelings and I didn't want that. I love my mom and I want to see her happy.

I know that its hard being a parent. You have a lot of responsibilities to take care of. You have to work and take care of your kids, make sure your kids don't turn out to be total failures in life. You have to teach them what's right and wrong. You have to stand by their sides through thick or thin. And sometimes you have to be strict with them or else they might be misled by their friends or, simply, peer pressure.

So I guess my parents aren't that bad after all. I understand why they are so strict. They love me and they want me to have a better future. They don't want me to fall into any peer pressure or do anything that is wrong, like drugs or getting pregnant. They want to see me live a happy and a successful life. They want me to have all the things in life that they never had or couldn't have. I still think that the arranged marriage issue is going too far but I guess I will just have to work around them. I am sure that when the time comes everything will be just fine. HOPEFULLY!

Tiffany Luu
English 098
Instructor: Fran Grimes

How I Got My Name 'Tiffany'

I went to Albion St. Elementary School. This school is located in Los Angeles. My kindergarten teacher was Mrs. Linda Wong. Mrs. Wong was a woman who was probably in her late forties or early fifties. Mrs. Wong was Chinese and spoke Cantonese fluently. She had a kind face which made it easy for me to go to her when I had problems.

There were fifteen people in my kindergarten class. I will always remember kindergarten where I played with sand boxes, hopscotch, dolls, monkey-bars, jungle-gyms, and toy stoves with pots and pans to play house. Life was easy back then. Days went by really fast in kindergarten. I didn't have to worry about adding, subtracting, multiplying and dividing. The hardest thing was learning my ABC'S. Everything else was easy.

I had lots of friends in my class. My closest friends were Maria, Julie, Christina, and Theresa. Although we were good friends, there was always something there that made me feel that I didn't belong in that group. For a while I thought it was because they all had older siblings and I didn't have any. I was the oldest child in the family. Then one day during recess, when we were sitting on top of the monkey-bars, Julie asked, "Why is your name Nhi? What does it mean?"

"Yeah! What does your whole name mean?" Christina added.

Theresa was always the one who made me feel inferior because she always brought those scratchy stickers that smelled like watermelon. She always stole the attention away from me. "Why don't you have an English name like we do?"

The sun seemed to be shining right at me, causing me to sweat. I could feel drops of sweat dripping down from my forehead. I hesitated for a while. "My name is Nhi Tiet Luu. In Chinese it's actually read backward. My name means Snow Child. 'Tiet' is snow, 'Nhi' is child and 'Luu' is my last name."

Theresa interrupted me and said, "Why don't you have an English name like we do?"

I had nothing against Theresa but a lot of times she got on my nerves. "I don't know why. I'll find out when I get home," I answered impatiently. "I just don't want to say anything anymore."

Luckily, Mrs. Wong rang the bell to let us know that recess was over. So we all jumped down from the monkey-bars and walked into the classroom. "How do you pronounce your name in Chinese?" Julie asked with a great big smile.

Julie was always nice to me, so I felt very comfortable. "Shuit Yee," I said.

"Oh!" Julie nodded. "It sounds very pretty."

The next day Mrs. Wong was absent. Mr. Martinez was our substitute. Mr. Martinez was a tall, handsome Hispanic man. The thing I didn't like about him was that he could not pronounce my name while he was taking the attendance. When he got to my name he said, "This is a little hard for me. Is it Tit Nhay?" The class started giggling.

"Teet Hi," Mr. Martinez continued and caused more laughing and giggling.

"Tiet Nhi, my name is Tiet Nhi," I corrected him.

"Oh yes, Tiet Nhi. I'm sorry Miss Luu." I blushed when he called me 'Miss Luu.' But I was not so happy when he mispronounced my name. I'd had it. I was sick of people mispronouncing my name. So I decided to go home and question my dad about my ugly name.

I remember that day I sat on the sofa, staring at the clock, waiting for the big hand to reach the six. My dad is a machinist and he gets off from work at 3:30 p.m. Right when the clock hit 3:30, I looked outside our apartment window and saw my dad's Oldsmobile pull in our parking lot. I rushed to open the door and waited for him to get comfortable. Then I waited patiently for him to change his working shoes into his favorite blue slippers and I waited till he sat on the sofa with a bunch of Chinese newspapers piled all over him. Then I knew it was time for me to burst out my question: "BaBa, why is my name Tiet Nhi? Why is our last name Luu instead of Garcia like Julie's last name or Martinez like Theresa's or Smith like Christina's?"

My father all of a sudden looked at me weirdly and continued reading his Chinese newspaper: "What's wrong, you don't like your name?"

I couldn't wait, and I blurted out why I didn't like my name, all at once. "Yeah, people mis-pronounce my name and my friends laugh at me. When Julie, Theresa, and Christina question me about my name, asking me why I don't have an English name, I don't even know what to tell them. My name sounds so awful in English. This is America and everyone has English names in America."

My father was still very patient with me and answered my questions: "Luu is our last name; we can't change our last name. This is something in our family that can never be changed. It's very special because it's the name of our whole entire family. It's your name, my name, your cousin's name, and aunt's name. Our family shares this name."

I was beginning to feel impatient and dissatisfied. That was not what I wanted to hear. I wanted him to say, "Okay, then we'll give you a new name." But he didn't say anything so I began to whine, "It still sounds bad. Then why is my name Tiet Nhi? It sounds so awful. People laugh and make fun of me 'cause of my name."

By this time my Dad had given me his undivided attention. He had gotten the newspaper out of his hand: "Tiet Nhi is just a translation of your Chinese name. If you want to have an English name just ask your teacher to give you an English name. I can't give you one because I don't know enough English to do so."

Now that was what I wanted to hear. I quickly answered my dad, "Okay, I'll ask Mrs. Wong tomorrow," and I skipped joyfully into my room and my dad went back to his newspaper.

The next day, while everyone was playing in the yard I stayed in the classroom to talk to Mrs. Wong. "Do you need something?" Mrs. Wong asked.

I told Mrs. Wong how much I didn't like my Chinese name because people couldn't pronounce it and how I felt that I didn't belong with Julie, Christina, and Theresa. "My dad asked if you can give me an English name," I shyly said, with my hands tightly folded together.

Mrs. Wong understood why I came to her for an English name because my mom had already talked to her about my little conversation with my father.

"Okay, just give me a couple of days and I'll give you an English name," Mrs. Wong said.

When I heard Mrs. Wong say that, I was so happy. I skipped outside to the playground to join my friends

On Wednesday morning, Mrs. Wong handed me a little piece of white paper folded in half. I opened it. The paper had 'Tiffany' written in black ink. "This is your new name. It's Tiffany. From now on your name is Tiffany."

From then on everyone called me Tiffany. At home my parents called me Tiffany or Nhi. My grandparents have trouble pronouncing Tiffany so they call me Nhi; my cousins call me Tiffany. Tiffany or Nhi, I'm still the same person.

Although I was raised here in America, just simply having an English name does not confuse me of who I am. I still have my own identity. Tiffany is just a name. I do not build my character based on my name. My Chinese name is very convenient for those who are not proficient English speakers. As for those who can speak English, they can address me as Tiffany.

What I am trying to convey is that my English name does not cause me to forget my heritage. Whether people address me as Tiffany or Tiet Nhi, I am still the same person. I'm a person filled with my Chinese tradition that was brought out by my family. I am also willing to adapt to the new culture that I learned here in America.

Tu Minh Tran
English 098
Instructor: Lynne Rosenberg

Leaving Vietnam

My parents made a great sacrifice when they migrated from North to South in search of a more fertile land in the 1950's. They had talked about their homeland of Nam Dinh and their little village where everyone was everyone's friend. Their homeland was prosperous and of old traditions. How about my homeland? Did I love Saigon? Would I ever leave Saigon for anywhere else? I was baffled with the questions. By the time I left Vietnam for America, my emigration experience helped me realize that I had loved my homeland relentlessly all along because of its human touch, its beauty, as well as its perseverance.

On August 15, 1988, an extraordinary event happened and changed our lives. The news came at last. We received a telegram from the Interior Department advising us to leave the country at 11:00 on Wednesday, September 4th, at Tan Son Nhat Airport--our destination: America. Our hearts were thrilled with every moment we put our thoughts to the dream land. For the first time, we felt we could breathe the air of freedom. For my father, who extremely detested the Communists, this was his victory. Eager for coming to America, we all shed a few tears of joy. The land of freedom and prosperity was awaiting us. America, here we come. At last...at last!

Then, the day of September 4th came knocking on our door. It was time for us to say good-bye to Vietnam and hello to America. As the red sun of dawn rose and merchants were flocking to Ban Co market to set off on their daily businesses, our neighbors gathered at 220 lot G to say good-bye and to wish us a safe trip. Mrs. Hue was among those people who cried and set off an emotional moment. My mom cried also. I understood my mom's feelings of estrangement because no one had so endured the turbulence of the migrating life which she owned, and now it recurred to her all over again. She left Vietnam for one reason, the future of her remaining three children. Looking up at my parents, I noticed my dad looked much older; and for my mom, gray hair started to streak her pearly-black hair.

Saigon was my childhood place. It possessed my memorable history with neighborhood kids, and so it possessed my heart. As much as I could remember, as children we were good kids and used to hang out on the strip of Dien Bien Phu Street to see the street lights, the vehicles, and the passers-by. Escaping the suffocating enclosure of the house to feel the breezy air of the wide-open boulevard, we talked of school, of bicycles, of dreams...of life. On the gloomy nights, we told ghost stories in the crime-infested alley, Ba Lon, with Nit, Nu, Na, and Nut, the four brothers with peculiar names. I was unable to say good-bye to them that morning because they all went to school, and I wished them the best and wondered how they would all have changed when I got back.

At 8:00 a.m., a Vietnam Airlines' bus approached our house and stirred up the crowd. Those who stayed behind gave their final farewell. All of the thirty people we had invited got on the bus, and we headed for the airport. The bus maneuvered through the bustling streets, honking vigorously at bicycles and scooters to arrogantly hustle them out of the way. Sitting on the bus, I tried to carefully recap the scenes of Saigon to remember what it looked like for the last time. I looked for memorable images to bring to America as a piece of my homeland in my heart. I saw shaggy houses, dirty streets and, most of all, the people laboring their way tirelessly to earn a living. My heart went out to those people and I wished that someday Vietnam would be free from Communism and thrive to be rich. The victory bus madly dashed through downtown Saigon where the most elegant civic buildings of Saigon, bearing their French Colonial architecture, stood sturdily. My brother and I used to hang out at this boastful municipal square where resided the Opera House, Ben Thanh Market, and the Due Ba Cathedral. But not long after that, the scene perpetuated itself. The slums of Saigon started reappearing along the Cuu Long River. The poverty-ridden houses looked old, broken, and run-down, revealing the irony of Communism. Vietnam, the Land of the Dragon, had been ravaged by many disasters--all of them were man-made. I hoped for peace and prosperity for the country.

At the airport, the air was stiff and got even stiffer as more and more people converged. I had never seen such a great mass of people. We found a spot far from the entrance to take refuge from the crowd. My brother's and sister's friends were very enthusiastic. My brother found himself becoming an instant star as many of his friends came. My friends, unfortunately, were unable to come because they had school. That was the reason that sister suddenly pulled me over to her side, along with her friends, to take pictures.

After that, while waiting patiently, I began to reflect on the memories I had with my friends. The most vivid memory I had about them was the picnic to Binh Thoi. We were invited by Viet's father to their country house. Our homeroom teacher, Ms. Lien, who had been with us since the sixth grade, coordinated the trip. This trip was memorable in the way we displayed our brotherhood, unity, and loyalty to one another. Most inspiring was the time when we gathered in a circle and sang aloud under the penetrating summer sun. We sang everything from country folk songs to the Communists' "I Love Uncle Ho," just for the irony of it. As we sang, our hearts harmonized and our spirits were uplifted. That trip also gave me the opportunity to explore the attractions of the country from which I discovered the hidden treasures of Vietnam, revealing itself in front of my eyes: the vibrancy of nature; the vast, golden rice fields racing with the wind like locks of lustrous hair; the muddy fish pond with its murky water; the deepest greenery, striking against the silky blue sky--the true meeting of heavenly beauty and earthy reality. These scenes mimicked Vietnam. But in a few moments I would leave this Asian Pearl for a new land and say farewell to everything I had lived and loved. The country I was bound for was America, the land of freedom and promise. I didn't quite understand the concept of "freedom" and "promise" but trusted my parents' words that America would be a better place for me.

At 11:00 a.m., the voice on the loud speakers urged passengers to check-in. We squeezed ourselves through the sweaty crowd. That was it. People cried to see people leave. There was a sentineled door. We stepped into it, and thus we were separated from our relatives and friends, knowingly forever. Freedom and prosperity were awaiting on one side; continuing oppression and poverty were left behind on another. My mom and my sister cried, looking at relatives through the glass windows. There were the joyful tears and the sorrowful ones; joy was for the freedom and sorrow was because of the estrangement. We could not say much because we were heart-broken. Everybody was sentimental, but I was strangely inert and indifferent. Disappearing into the custom booth, I waved at my relatives.

At 1:00 p.m., we got on the plane. When the voice from the plane's intercom started to say, "Good afternoon, ladies and gentlemen...," it was time for us to depart. On the plane, to catch a glimpse of my relatives for the last time, I tried to spot the red umbrella that my sister brought, but there were about a dozen red umbrellas. As the twin propellers of the Russian-made Tupolev roared their high-pitched, wind-shearing sound, I started to cry. Tears were warming my cheeks in profusion and I tried to conceal them from my family who had now turned calm and mellow. The setting made me feel alone with my thoughts as if no one was sharing my feelings. Then I really felt the effects of it all. Only at that moment did I realize that everything was real and that I was not hallucinating; I was actually leaving my country. All my thoughts turned into tears as I sobbed quietly. Those solemn tears told all about the experience of a fifteen year-old boy who had emigrated from his country. The plane soared high and kept on climbing; when I looked down, the city got smaller and turned miniature. I said farewell to Vietnam in spirit. On my shoulders, I carried with me a heavy burden: the promise for a better future for Vietnam, the sorrow of leaving the country, and the uncertainty going to a new land.

Leaving Vietnam was not a celebrating moment for me. But now, whenever I think about that time, I am glad I had such a feeling when I left my country. It is a beautiful reminder of who I was and where I came from. Whenever I think of that event, I remember the faces of my relatives and my friends more vividly. Living a different life in America, I will never forget Vietnam: the place, the people, the culture. For the time being, life has not been so bad for me in America. I am going to college and can expect a bright future when I graduate. I will stay in America for the rest of my life but would like to return to Vietnam and work alongside the people there to help rebuild the country.

*The test of literature is, I suppose, whether we
ourselves live more intensely for the reading of it.*
Elizabeth Drew

Sergio Miramontes--Honorable Mention
English 098
Instructor: Emily Lawsin

El Coyote

My trip to the United States started with one question, *"Quieres ver a tu papa?"* My mother, with a bright face, asked me if I wanted to see my father. He was in the United States already and we were going to live with him. The next thing I knew we were on a plane to Tijuana. Some things from the experience are not clear, as I was seven at the time, but other things are as clear as crystal. We came into the country illegally, so we crossed *por el serro,* through the mountains.

When we began to cross *el serro,* we started by crossing over a wire fence, down the sloped banks into a small river or canyon. At that time, from the people who surrounded me, a feeling began creep over me, as if we were doing something that wasn't allowed. We had a guide, or *el coyote,* and he gave us instructions on what to do. A group of about fifteen people stood in the canyon behind *el coyote* on a rough cliff, in our path a bent and broken gate. *El coyote* said, *"Aqui hay cholos. Agarren piedras y hechenlas en la bolsa."* With these words, people began to pick rocks off the floor. I filled my pockets and carried more in my hands. As I gripped them with the strength of fear, the edges of the roughest rocks hurt my hands. The gate dormant on the floor, we walked through.

We followed *el coyote* through a forest and came to a river. He said, *"Ya pueden tirar las piedras. P'aca ya no hay cholos."* The people let go of the rocks that weighed them down. I let go of only the ones in my hands. The fresh, cool relief in my palms ran to the tips of my fingers, but the weight in my pockets never changed. The river, a sight full of beauty, wasn't deep, but the sands and banks were bright golden brown, the colors of green and brown running along the banks. *"El rio esta seco en este tiempo, pero cuidado que no se hunda la arena,"* warned *el coyote.* A line of people began to cross the dry river where the banks were at their lowest. At that point, every feeling inside of me swelled. That beautiful river suddenly became a river full of uncertainty, and I was unsure if something would happen under my feet. I stepped on the sand and crossed the river full of darkness. I didn't say a word. I kept alert of what was around me. We began to cross another field, in line behind *el coyote.* We were walking on a dirt road, a field of wheat-like plants with trees a few yards away on the right side, trees on the left side, another road crossing ours a few yards ahead. It was silent but for the subtle sounds of movement, that of each foot-step. With anxiety on his face, *el coyote* exclaimed, *"Tirense entre las yerbas y no salgan hasta que les diga!"*

The people fell to the right. *El coyote* ducked into the plants, the feet of the death-like bodies sticking out of the plants, and on the road ahead, a truck drove by. In my left ear, the sound of friction, like the legs of a pair of pants rubbing against each other with each step, as the wind blews and moved the plants. In my right ear, the sound of the tires crushing the dirt under their weight. The wind whistled silently in both my ears. My unsure hands fringed my pockets. In whispers, *"La migra! La migra!"* El coyote went and looked to see if the truck was gone, and then he came back. His voice with urgency said, *"Vamos a cruzar la carretera, pero vallanse agachados y pronto pa' que no los vean!"* Too young to understand what was happening and old enough to be afraid, I was like a well-trained soldier. Without understanding and without thought, I acted on what I was told. In groups of two, with our legs and backs bent, we ran across the road into a field of tall and thin plants. The field seemed a swamp; trash on the floor, a dirty diaper, and an empty gallon stayed in my mind. A field of bamboo, harboring within it a cluster of people, keeping low, waiting for the rest to cross, their hot, hard breath like that of tired runners. Now my hands were in my pockets, with the all too well-remembered feel of a rock's edge. My Uncle saw I still had the rocks in my pocket and took them out. He laughed, perhaps he needed to, but I had been ready for what might happen. I remained as alert as ever.

We kept on going and entered a new field. This one had tall green trees and the floor was carpeted with luscious green plants. It was dark by now and that added to the beauty. It was like a small forest or jungle and yet, a distance away, I could see a small barren area. Across the area some type of wire, a fence, and on the other side of the fence was where a large, dark, paved lot began. On the lot was a pale van. That was our goal, the van. *"El Mosko! El Mosko! "* shouted *el coyote.* The bodies once again fell into the green plants and under the trees. The presence of a monster, an enemy, a giant insect, a giant mosquito was felt just behind the trees and as it flew overhead, my eyes couldn't look up. The sound of its wings flapping seemed to fill the earth. *El coyote's* trembling eyes turned to the people, his voice full of anxiety saying, *"No dejen que les pege la luz!"* A man under a tree squirmed to avoid being hit by the light. My wide eyes followed the light, the light that somehow meant sudden death to everyone. We remained there, waiting for *El Mosko* to go away. In our sight was the van. In the darkness it was finally decided that it was time to go to the van. A man went first; everybody watched. He ran, reached the fence, and tangled it so it would be easier to cross. He remained there as groups of two or so ran to the fence and then to the van. In my mind, the journey from that point to the van is a blank. At times I can still hear that moment and see the people moving in my mind. The next thing I remember is being in the warm, dark, safety of the van.

Once in the van, something happened that I will never forget. There was another van there and it got full, so an old lady was sent to our van. She talked to one of the men in charge. I listened to her timid voice; she said, *"El otro van esta lleno. Mi hijo me dijo que me fuera con Ustedes."*

The man in charge said, *"No, no. Nosotros tambien estamos llenos. Ya no tenemos cupo."*

The expression on her face turned to fear, *"Pero mi hijo ya se fue."*

The man's now irritated voice said, *"Mire senora . Ya le dije que no!"*

Another man then said, **"Porque no deja que se vaya con nosotros?"**

The man in charge, pushing his authority, said, *"Te quieres quedar tu?"* The man, fearing being left behind, sat back down.

Once the old lady had left, the man in charge turned to the people in the van and said, *"Ven! Por eso no me gusta pasar viejitas."* The people looked for his reason, but there was none, and laying on the crowded floor, the curtains closed, left on their way. I don't know what happened to that old lady, but I felt a white-haired, defenseless, frail, old woman was left behind in a large, dark sea, full of uncertainty.

That night we stayed in a house that was close by. From there all the people were to be taken to their destinations and *el coyote* would collect his fee. That day *el coyote* started to make his deliveries. That night I arrived in my new home. I walked up the walkway that led to the front door. Cement on the floor, a large glass window on the right, a window in front, on the left many small trees, and next to the large window stood the front door. That night everything looked brilliant, new, lively, and exciting. The next morning my family went to buy food and I saw the street on the other side of the house. It looked like the walkway--brilliant. That brilliance disappeared in a day and it has never looked that beautiful again.

Let's face it, writing is hell.
William Styron

Sarkis Aznavour
English 098
Instructor: Eve Caram

A Trip To Lebanon

After an eighteen-hour flight the pilot came on the intercom and said in Arabic, "Fasten your seat belts because we are on our final descent." After anticipating this moment for months, we were finally there. I looked out the window and saw nothing but buildings crowded together. Considering that there had been fifteen years of civil war, I was surprised at how many buildings there were. When we landed, everyone clapped and the pilot came on the intercom and said, "Welcome to Beirut, Lebanon."

After intensely planning where we would go for vacation, my parents had picked Lebanon because the war had ended, because they had not been there for a long time, and because we had family there that we had never seen. We also chose Lebanon because my parents had always said it was a beautiful country and they wanted us to see how life was halfway across the world. So for the summer of 1990 we went to Lebanon, a place like no other in the world.

My parents were born in Lebanon and lived there for eighteen years, and they moved out only because the civil war had started. They had just finished high school when they left Lebanon, so when we went to Lebanon we did not have to worry about having problems with the language because in Lebanon students are required to learn Arabic, French, English, and if you happen to be Armenian, then you learn Armenian as well.

When we entered the terminal at Beirut International Airport, everything was either written in Arabic or French. There was no air conditioning like we have here at American airports, and the weather was very sticky and humid. It felt like we had just got out of a steam bath. When we went to get our baggage, we saw people with rusted old carts waiting to help the people who had just got off the plane. After getting our baggage we were supposed to go to get our bags checked by the airport police. But because my uncle had connections, we were escorted out of the airport without even a luggage check.

When we finally got out of the airport, we had about twenty people or so waiting for us. It was pretty crazy having all these people hug and kiss us on our cheeks when we did not even know who they were. But later in our vacation I realized that hugging and kissing was a tradition used by Arabs and some Europeans to show affection. After all the commotion, we got into different cars and headed to my aunt's apartment in Antillias, a suburb about fifteen kilometers north of Beirut. As we went through the war-torn country, we saw abandoned buildings with bullet holes, we saw buildings with their floors hanging because of missiles that had come through them, and we saw trash burning in the streets. In some of these buildings, Palestinian refugees lived for free because the owners had left to save their own lives. As we drove through downtown Beirut, we realized what war can do to a nation. Some of the streets were like ghost streets with nothing to see but holes through the walls of the buildings. As we looked around, a chill ran up my spine and I saw my mother had tears in her eyes. Some of our relatives told us of how the war had affected them--sometimes they had to go fifteen days without taking a shower because they had no running water. Sometimes two groups of people would get into a fight with each other, each group would kill people on the other side, but at the end the two who were fighting would act as if there had never been a fight between them. A country once considered as the Switzerland of the Middle East, because of its beauty and prosperity, was now the most chilling country to be in.

As we got on the Autostrat, which was Lebanon's freeway, I wondered how these people drove. There were no lanes, no police officers, and yet in the month and a half that we drove, we didn't see any accidents. People honked their horns, zigzagged through traffic and in some places through holes in the street where bombs had fallen. I did drive a moped there a few times, but when I heard there were a lot of motorcycle accidents, I left driving to the people who had experience with it.

While in Lebanon, we stayed at my aunt's apartment which was pretty big. As in Europe and in most countries of the world, except for the United States, people live in seven to eight story apartment buildings that have two families per floor. There are no houses in the cities, only in less populous places like the mountains. During the day we usually went to the beaches. But the beaches in Lebanon are not like the beaches here; they are all private and have swimming pools and tennis courts; guests are given private rooms to store things in and change. My uncle and aunt took us to the beach because they had membership at one of the beaches. At night we would go to Jebel, the name given to the mountains of Lebanon, only a twenty-minute drive from the city. In the mountains, people acted as if there had never been a war. Wearing Chanel clothes, they drove up in their Mercedes SL's and sat at tables and spent a few hundred dollars on drinks and food. Most of the people at these restaurants were Lebanese who had fled during the civil war. They had become successful business men in Europe and the United States and now that the war had ended in Lebanon, they were back to rebuild the country with the money they had made from the outside world. The main reason people went to Jebel was because of the excellent food, service, cool weather, and the view of the Mediterranean. The view of the ocean is what really stuck in my mind. Wherever we went up the mountain we could see the sparkling Mediterranean Sea.

One day my uncle took us to the ancient Roman city of Baalbek, a two-hour drive from the city of Beirut. When we got to Baalbek, I was amazed at how big the ancient Roman columns were. The columns were about five stories high, made of granite and brought from Egypt. As we headed back to Beirut, we saw posters of devils with the Star of David behind them. The Posters were put up for propaganda against Jews in the security zone in the south of Lebanon, by Hezbollah, a terrorist group that was stationed in Baalbek.

As we boarded the plane to come to the United States, my brother and mother had tears in their eyes because of the memories we would have of this great summer. When we got home I realized how spoiled we Americans had become. We do not live in a country that has had a recent fifteen-year war, we always have electricity and hot water, and we have the opportunity to become whatever we want. But in spite of all that, we usually have something to complain about every day of our lives.

Tafesse Alemu
English 098
Instructor: Marilyn Segal

Yes, it's hard to write, but it's harder not to.
Carl Van Doren

Easter Holiday Celebration in Ethiopia

There is one tradition in particular that I grew fond of as a child. It is the way in which Easter was celebrated in Ethiopia. The Easter holiday is the most important religious holiday that is observed in the Ethiopian Coptic Orthodox Christian Community. Traditionally, people prepare for the coming of the Easter holiday months ahead. Easter is the day on which our God, Jesus Christ, ascended from death to the heavens above. It is a day of reflecting on the three important values of love, sacrifice, and forgiveness. For most, it is a time of affirmation of God's Covenant. So, the amount of energy that it takes in preparing for the holiday is enormous. Most devoted followers avoid luxuries and fast for forty days before the holiday. Their meals during the fast consist of vegetables and grains. Some even fast with only water and bread for most of the period. People usually recite verses from the Bible, chant, and meditate in private. There is a deep traditional aspect to the way we celebrate Easter in Ethiopia.

There is always commotion the day before Easter in most people's houses. In our house, people get up early in the morning. My father goes to the shepherds a few miles from our house, to select the sheep to be slaughtered for this special occasion. He also goes to a chicken farm to buy two or more chickens. Usually, he hires a laborer that has experience in slaughtering the animals according to the specifications of the cook, my mother. All of these things occur during the morning hours of the day. The ladies of the house spend most of the day preparing all the traditional meals to be served. It is common for them to make five to ten different dishes of food to be served. They also spend time baking huge loaves of bread in the stone ovens. Months before Easter, they prepare two different types of fermented liquors. One is made out of fermented barley and the other is made from fermented honey. The ladies also spend time filtering the liquor drinks in lightly woven cotton cloths. Chairs are removed from the dining room area and they are replaced with traditional stool chairs. The table is replaced with a round straw table/tray that is slightly higher than the stool chairs. Dry alfalfa or straws of grass are spread all over the dining-room floor. There are also leaves that are dispersed on the living-room floor, giving the most beautiful smell. The different aromas that fill the house will remind me of the Easter holidays as long as I live.

In the late afternoon everyone goes to rest, knowing that they will have to attend the church procession at 9:00 p.m.. When the time for the church procession nears, everyone gets up and gets ready. It is traditional to wear white cotton garments for church. The ladies wear long dresses that come down to their ankles and light cloths to cover their heads. The men wear cotton pants and skirts with side slits. The ladies also carry a few loaves of bread, some honey liquor, and some barley liquor. Most people don't drive because there are churches in all the neighborhoods. Since there are few city lights, the streets are pitch dark. The only other lights come from the moon and the stars. All the neighbors walk harmoniously to the church. The old men and women carry staffs to lean on for the long church service. On reaching the church gates, people kiss the ground and the huge crosses on the gates. They proceed walking to the church door and on reaching the door, they kiss the floor and the ground again. Then, before entering the church, they all take off their shoes.

The church procession begins as soon as the church is full. Most of the sermon is done in the church language called Geze. It was a spoken language once, before becoming obsolete (except in churches). The church service involves chanting, prayers, and preaching by the priest. We all stand during most of the service. The church is full of beautiful icons and drawings. There are incense stones burning all around that give a smell that energizes the room. The priest gives most of the sermon behind curtains in the front of the congregation. The monks lead most of the procession. The service lasts until two or three in the morning. At the end of the service, the priest blesses each individual. As we exit the door, we kiss the cross which the priest holds out. Then, feeling good but tired, we head home.

After assembling inside the house, the ladies leave the men to warm the food they had spent preparing all day. Most of us are pretty hungry and tired. As soon as the food is prepared, we all gather next to the single huge plate on which we will break the fast. The father of the house prays out loud as we eat. After the meal, the ladies roast some coffee on a metal plate and burn the incense on a clay cup. They grind the coffee using a steel club and a wooden cup. Then they brew the coffee and serve the bread prepared in the early parts of the day. Everyone sleeps after they have eaten.

The Easter holidays I have spent as a child will remain meaningful and delightful in my heart forever. A large part of what we are today reflects on the ways we were raised and molded. People in the world today are as heterogeneous as their different shades represent. We come from numerous cultures filled with rich histories. No one culture is greater than the other, even though it seems that way to some with dominating cultures. Each one of us is very sentimental and comfortable with our cultures. For me, the Easter Holidays I have spent exemplify the way I was raised. I came from a family that believed in togetherness and that was the way we spent the holidays--together. The most important ingredient that made Easter more special to me was the simple fact that we were all there. In the church procession we were together. In the morning hours when we broke the fast, we were together. Sometimes I really miss the voices that gathered around the table. Some of them have died and some are far away. I miss my mother's cooking and my father's blessing before we eat. Although I live in America, which is by far the richest country in the world, there are some things that it doesn't have to make my Easter celebration as fulfilling as when I was young.

Every year I try to improvise with what I have. When I am married and have children, I want to create the joy my parents shared with me on Easter. I want them to understand the importance of family. I don't want to make it as superficial as Christmas is becoming. My kids will fast for the duration of the forty days before Easter, like I did. They will also break the fast, like I did, after attending church service. Easter should be a mixture of festivity and profound religious experience. They should be happy because of Easter and pass on the tradition to their offspring.

Text-Based
Essays

Cindy Hemmings--Honorable Mention
English 097
Instructor: Sandra Jackson

A Moral Lesson

What is a parable? It's a question that we may all ask. It's a wake-up call to get up and smell the coffee. It's a door that slams in your face, leaving an ugly scar behind. It's a ghost that hunts you down until it takes you to the other end. It's a mother that tries to teach the difference between right and wrong. A parable is a short and simple story teaching a moral lesson; a lesson to be learned. Ready or not, it's coming straight at you and it's about to hit you, even though you don't want to realize it. *The Pearl* by John Steinbeck is a short story, but it has the meaning of fire. The fire that burns your heart and makes you beg for forgiveness. It's the desire to have the power to turn time back and listen to what others have to say, putting your guard down and pride aside.

The message that *The Pearl* brings is not easy to explain in a few words. It's a message that has not one, but many meanings. It makes you realize how a person's attitude towards life can change in a split second when faced with an opportunity or a chance to succeed in an ironic way. It's when death, hatred and greed are at your tail and out to get you. It makes you forget who you are, who you love, and even what makes you happy. At the beginning of the story, Kino and his family were poor, but they were happy with what they had. Kino felt that his life was composed of songs expressing the way he interpreted life. Every morning when he woke up, the song of family would play in his mind. His wife lay in bed next to him with her eyes open, waiting for him to open his. She would get up in her bare feet and check on Coyotito. Then she would cook their usual breakfast of corncake and *pulque*. Then Kino got up and slipped his feet into his sandals and he went outside to see the beautiful Gulf wake up. Kino didn't know that the evil song would knock on his door (which was waiting to be opened) and be ready to strike. Coyotito, the family's baby, was struck by a scorpion, and the evil song had come to stay. Juana sucked the poison out, but they weren't sure if Coyotito would live. They took the baby to the doctor, but the doctor would not help them because Kino had no money to pay for the treatment. In desperate need, Kino and Juana went slowly down to the beach to Kino's canoe. The canoe had great value to Kino, because it was passed down to him from his grandfather. Kino was looking for the song of the pearl that might be. They sailed and Kino went under the water and gathered many shells. When he climbed into the canoe, he started to open the shells. Suddenly BOUMmmm!! There it was, the great pearl. Kino was introduced not only to the pearl, but to the answer to his prayers, and he was also introduced to death, hatred, and greed. That's the point where Kino forgot who he was, who he loved, and even what made him happy.

Another message that *The Pearl* has is that money can't buy happiness. You can compare Kino with the doctor who didn't want to treat Coyotito. On one hand is Kino, a man who is poor, but he is surrounded by the love of his family. On the other hand is the doctor, who was in a good position compared to Kino: "In the chamber the doctor sat in his high bed." He was wearing a gown of red watered silk from Paris that was tight over his chest because he was fat. In his lap was a silver tray with a silly china cup that he could not even lift with his big hand. He was surrounded by religious pictures and a large photograph of his dead wife, which made him remember France and his mistress: "That was civilized living." But the doctor was not happy at all; instead he was looking for the love that Kino had in his material possessions, and the only things that he found were loneliness and sadness inside his heart.

This leads me to my next point, which is that money corrupts people and they don't realize what they have until they lose it. Even though Kino was a happy man, he took for granted what he had, and the pearl became his soul. He became a fugitive, a murderer, and an evil man. For example, when Juan asked Kino to throw the pearl away because it was destroying his family, he just ignored her. There was no way that he would throw the pearl away. Juana got up early the next morning and she went to throw the pearl back from where it came, but Kino caught her. "He struck her in the face with his clenched fists." She was the only person by his side and he hurt her, not only physically but also emotionally. Another example is when Kino became a fugitive, followed by three men in the desert because they wanted the pearl. Unfortunately, little Coyotito was killed in the process. The cry of death had come, and the evil song was still playing. That's when Kino finally opened his eyes and saw what he had done to his family and how the pearl had corrupted him. He had to lose what he loved and what made him happy and it was too late to fix it. Kino had to lose something in order to gain something. He lost his son and he gained his old self again. The family song was alive now.

Another meaning of *The Pearl* is that we tend to see only the outside instead of the inside, which is what really matters. Kino was amazed by the beautiful pearl, the pearl of success, prosperity and hope. He saw only the size of the pearl, the beautiful incandescent colors and the bright light that the pearl projected from the outside. Kino never paid attention to the true meaning that the pearl had stored for him: the size that grew into evil and hate, the color that turned into gray and the bright light that turned into darkness.

The character that I relate to the most in this story is Juana. At the beginning of the story, Steinbeck shows Juana as the follower, her obedient and inferior side. You can almost picture Juana waiting aside for Kino to finish eating in order for her to eat. She always had to do what her husband told her to do, but at the end everything changes. When Juana and Kino come back from the desert, they walk side by side, not in a single file as before. They go to the beach and they throw the pearl into the water. Juana never had a doubt in her mind about what to do. Kino realized that Juana was right all along and how important she was to him. To me, Juana was the real hero in the story, the hero behind the door, the hero who loved her family over all, even herself.

My last point is how primitive and modern society relate to one another. People tend to be greedy and jealous when they see other people's fortunes. They burned Kino's house, they destroyed his canoe, and they got him out of town. The only time that the whole town grew interested in Kino was when he found the pearl. Even the doctor and the priest changed their attitudes towards Kino, trying to take his fortune away. I believe that if this story took place in today's society, the exact same thing would happen, and maybe even worse. At the end of the story, Kino was a completely different person. A man who had learned a moral lesson, which left a scar for life, a scar that would make him realize the true meaning of love and how money can change a person's life in a split second. What would I do if I were in Kino's shoes? Would I be as brave as Juana, always knowing what to do, or would I make the same mistakes that Kino made? This is something that is very hard to answer. Probably I will never find the right answers to these questions, but at least I can understand what Kino went through. He was not a hero, but he was not a fool either. After all, we are all human and we make mistakes. The pearl is a malignant cancer that grows inside each one of us. It is a cancer that is eating us alive, little by little. We have to stop it from eating us and try to take it out of our systems before it's too late. The song of evil is at the door. Ready or not, it's coming straight at you and it's about to hit you.

The unread story is not a story;
it is little black marks on wood pulp.
The reader, reading it makes it live; a live thing, a story.
Ursula K. Le Guin

Cristina Rosales
English 098
Instructor: Eve Caram

Growing Up Is Hard To Do

A child grows up to learn right from wrong and to take on responsibilities. Maturity is clearly depicted in the novel, *When the Rainbow Goddess Wept*, written by Cecilia Manguerra Brainard. This novel is about a young girl's life as she grows up in the Philippines during World War II. When the story opens, the Japanese Invasion forces her and her family to leave their home. As the story unfolds we, as readers, see how Yvonne Macaraig, the main character, matures into a strong young woman.

Yvonne matures rapidly in several instances when she has to make the choice of putting her own wishes aside in order to take care of others. She is also able to find an inner strength, with the help of the family's cook, Laydan. Through Laydan and her stories, Yvonne is able to console and encourage herself during the war: "Then I thought that what Laydan would have really wanted me to do was to tell one of her stories....To ease my grief and to honor Laydan..." (94-5).

Part of growing up and maturing is learning the cycle of life and death. Yvonne begins to learn when she meets Doc Meñez. Doc Meñez had just lost his family. The Japanese soldiers massacred them and Yvonne's family is obligated to take him with them when they come across his residence. During the time when Doc Meñez grieved over the massacre, Yvonne took care of him. No one had told her to do this, but her curiosity about Doc caused her to follow through: "I checked on him periodically, watching his chest rise and fall to make sure he was still breathing" (83). Another instance in which Yvonne learns more about death is when her mother asks her to watch over Cristobal Alvarez, Gil Alvarez's eleven-year old son. Cristobal is the only child who survived his family's massacre. Just like Doc Meñez, Cristobal is also in a state of shock and then developed an oddness in his lifestyle: "I disliked Cristobal Alvarez, but Mama had told me to watch him....Since the Japanese killed his mother and four brothers and sisters, he started eating mud" (143-4). Although Yvonne was younger, her role made her older. She had to act in a mature way in order for Cristobal to behave realistically. She made sure that he was not getting himself into trouble and followed him wherever he went. Yvonne told Cristobal some of Laydan's stories in order for him to stay occupied and avoid trouble.

Aside from learning the cycle of life and death, in order for Yvonne to become mature she needs to find out who she really is and what she will become. As she reaches puberty, her femininity begins to emerge. When she takes care of Nida's newborn baby girl, she begins to learn and develop motherly qualities: "I took the baby away. I was jiggling her on my shoulders, trying to pacify her" (178). Another instance is when she is forced to take care of her mother and the others.

Nida and her Mama had quarreled and were not on talking terms so that Yvonne had no choice but to take over the situation. Even though she hated killing the family's chickens, when she regarded them as friends, she had no other option but to have the chickens slaughtered for food: "I stared at her with a shocked expression. We can't do that...they're like--like relatives" (157). "I told the men to catch her and kill her....I told myself there was no choice, no choice whatsoever, we needed food" (185). Yvonne was on her own. With her father gone and Doc Meñez searching for him, she was the mistress of their domain. Who else could keep the house in good condition, but Yvonne? Although her Mama and Nida were ignoring her efforts, she made sure that everyone was well and safe, and she kept the faith within them that her father and the others would return.

At this point in the novel, Yvonne has turned eleven and she and her family are back into their liberated city. Her father is back; she and her family have returned to the city and are faced with a different life. The most obvious sign of maturity is when she gets her first period: "I felt a stomach cramp. The pain was sharp...I noticed bloodstains" (201). She calls out to her mother when she sees blood. She thinks she is wounded but finds out that she has begun to menstruate. After that incident, Yvonne begins to recognize the possible physical, mental and emotional changes within her. She realizes that she is no longer a child but a woman: "For that was what a woman did. And I, my mother had just said, was now a woman" (202).

This novel clearly shows how Yvonne's hardships and experiences during the war has shaped her into a strong-willed young woman. She has learned about life and maturity at an early age. Within years, at the age of thirteen, we see that she has grown more that most do throughout their teenage years. All of us can relate to this kind of growth but need a much longer period to achieve it.

As a young adult going into my last year as a "teenager," I have experienced quite an adventure as well. One experience, or should I say "obstacle," I could definitely classify as a "fast maturity," was when my family and I had to move to Los Angeles from the Philippines. To others it may not seem to be such a big deal, but it is. To live in a new place, a whole new country, was not very easy, especially at the age of thirteen. Just like Yvonne, I also had to adjust to our new life. I had to take on responsibilities such as cooking for the family, caring for the house, etc.. There were new responsibilities that I had to add to my schedule. Our life here compared to our life back in the Philippines is so different. In the Philippines we had people who worked for my family to take care of the house and chores. Besides this work, I, too, had to take charge when my parents were struggling with the financial burden. While my brother was still adjusting to our new lives, I had to put my life on hold and be the first child in the family to work. Not only do I think that all of us go through some kind of experience that matures us, but I also know that in our hearts we know these experiences help us to learn.

Emilda Generalao
English 098
Instructor: Colleen Schaeffer

What's in a Title?

After reading the novel *Obasan* by Joy Kogawa, I was left questioning why exactly the title had been *Obasan*, since the book was about a Japanese-Canadian family, the Nisei, and mainly Naomi. Throughout the story Naomi is remembering memories of her past when faced with the death of her uncle. She remembers what hardships World War II brought to her family and the struggle to keep the family together and alive. All the Japanese-Canadian families' properties were taken away: "Seizure and government sale of fishing boats. Suspension of fishing licenses. Relocation camps. Liquidation of property. Deportation. Revocation of Nationality" (40). This was the harsh history that all the Japanese living in Canada had to undergo and endure.

The two main characters in the novel, besides Naomi, were Aunt Emily and Obasan. One presumption of the title, before I started reading the book, was to mark that the book was about Obasan, one of Naomi's aunts, but the book was about Naomi, her life and her mystery.

In Canada, throughout World War II, Naomi's mother was not there to shelter her; instead her aunts were there for her. They became Naomi's maternal role models. Obasan was primarily there to take care of Naomi, while Aunt Emily was an activist and deeply associated with fighting for justice for Japanese-Canadian citizens: "Whether she's dealing with the Japanese-Canadian issue or woman's rights or poverty, she's one of the world's white blood cells, rushing from trouble spot to trouble spot with her medication pouring into the wounds seen and not seen" (41).

Obasan was quite the opposite of Aunt Emily: "Obasan is very gentle and quiet like Naomi's mother" (81). Throughout Naomi's childhood, Obasan is there, giving her shelter, providing her with the right food and clothing. Obasan cares very much for Naomi, though she is not one for hugs and kisses.

As Naomi grew up she looked up to her aunts for help and guidance, but does the title *Obasan* signify the gratitude given to her Aunt Obasan or, since the title "Obasan" is used in the Japanese to mean "aunt," does the title show gratitude towards both aunts?

At one point in the book her aunts received a very important and saddening letter about Naomi's mother, but they decided not to tell her. They said, "Kodomo no tame--for the sake of the children" and "gaman shi masho--let us endure" (294), which suggests they did this out of love for Naomi and for her own good. They didn't tell her about the letter also because her mother wished them not to tell her.

Because Naomi was so young when they received the letter and because they were worried about how Naomi would handle the news about her mother, they didn't tell her until she was older and mature enough to handle the information. Upon her Uncle's death, when Naomi is older, they read her a letter sent from Naomi's grandmother that is dated back to the time when the atomic bomb was dropped, which was the time when Naomi's mother was in Japan caring for her sister. After the bomb fell, her grandma did not know where Nesan, Naomi's mother, was.

One evening when she had given up the search for the day, she sat down beside a naked woman she'd seen earlier who was aimlessly chipping wood to make a pyre on which to cremate a dead baby. The woman was utterly disfigured. Her nose and one cheek were almost gone. Great wounds and pustules covered her entire face and body. She was completely bald. She sat in a cloud of flies, and maggots wriggled among her wounds. As her grandma watched her, the woman gave her a vacant gaze, then let out a cry. It was Naomi's mother. She was taken to a hospital and expected to die. For a long time she wore bandages on her face. After they were removed she felt her face, then asked for a cloth mask which she wore and never took off (286). Discovering this helps Naomi reach an understanding in her life. This knowledge helps her to connect to the mother she never knew, and actually to bond with her, even though she wasn't physically there. Naomi realizes that it was good that her aunts had not told her when she was younger because she wouldn't have understood and there would have been no connection to her mother.

Since Naomi finally reaches harmony in her life because of both aunts, I am led to my assumption that Joy Kogawa entitled her novel *Obasan* because of Naomi's aunts and the role they played in the novel. They were key to resolving Naomi's mystery about her mother. I truly enjoyed the story but it left me thinking of how I would've felt if my mother were not with me throughout my life and my aunts didn't tell me the whole story until many years after I had grown up. I would probably be happy to finally know the mystery about my mother's whereabouts, but by the next day I would probably be in their faces asking them as many questions as I possibly could, to find out if there was any more information about my mother that they hadn't told me.

Thuc Duy Phan--Honorable Mention
English 097
Instructor: Eve Caram

The Impermanence of Life

Life constantly flows like the changing current of a river. Nothing is permanent in this life. Everyone is dissatisfied with this change of life. Everyone has to face aging and death as a process of change, but feels unhappy about it. People try to cling to something that may make them happy. However, there is no permanent thing to cling to. This makes the dissatisfaction become greater. This is the main theme of the short novel, *Siddhartha*. Although Siddhartha is also dissatisfied with the changes in the life process, he finally attains peace.

Siddhartha is the son of a Brahmin, the highest cast, wealthy and noble. This implies that he has plenty of respect, and material comfort. However, he feels dissatisfied with himself. This dissatisfaction is clearly indicated in the passage:

> But Siddhartha himself was not happy. Wandering along the rosy path of the fig garden, sitting in contemplation in the bluish shade of the grove, washing his limbs in the daily bath atonement, offering sacrifices in the depth of shady mango wood with the grace of manner, beloved by all, a joy to all, there was yet no joy in his own heart. (5)

Of course, what he feels is a true thing. In the past, many rulers or wealthy people were unhappy even though they had plenty of wealth and respect. This is the reason why people say that money cannot buy happiness. For us, the common people who do not always get what we want, the dissatisfaction is even greater.

Furthermore, people may think that having knowledge will satisfy them. However, after many centuries, people are still unhappy. Even knowledgeable people are still unhappy. They constantly look for new kinds of knowledge to fill their dissatisfaction. This is also the case for Siddhartha in following passage:

> He had begun to suspect that his worthy father and his teachers, the wise Brahmins, had already passed on to him the bulk and the best of their wisdom, that they had already poured the sum total of their knowledge into his waiting vessel; and his vessel was not full, his intellect was not satisfied, his soul was not at peace, his heart was not still. (5)

The Samanas think that destroying the senses will bring happiness. They believe that they have feelings because of the activities of the senses. They think if they kill the senses, they will no longer have feeling and will no longer feel unhappy. With the same belief, Siddhartha has left his family to become a Samana (12). He practices meditation and self-denial such as fasting for twenty-eight days, crouching among the thorns, standing under the rain and cold weather, etc.. Still, he cannot find happiness. Here is Siddhartha's thinking:

> We shall grow old...and do exercises, fast, meditate, but we will not attain
> Nirvana...I believe that amongst all the Samanas, probably not even one will
> attain Nirvana. (18)

Then Siddhartha leaves the Samanas to see the Buddha. He attends the Buddha's teachings but he cannot feel satisfied, and he leaves the Buddha. This time, he seeks the experiences of love's pleasure from women and he seeks wealth in the common life. However, he is never satisfied with these experiences, despite the fact that many people want to have them.

Throughout his life Siddhartha frequently faces dissatisfaction or unhappiness. Why does Siddhartha feel happy at the end when he sees the river? The first time he wakes himself from dissatisfaction is the time he realizes the true power of the Om (89). The Om is a holy word that means "Perfect One" or "Perfection" (89). This suggests that his inner self is already perfect because the Om, Perfection, comes from within his inner self, as revealed in this passage:

> Then from a remote part of his soul, from the past of his tired life, he heard a
> sound. It was one word, one syllable, which without thinking he spoke
> indistinctly, the ancient beginning and the ending of all Brahmin prayers, the holy
> Om.... (89)

Now, he realizes that his action is "folly" because he has spent his life looking for a perfection from without rather than from within (89). The wealth, respect, knowledge, practice of self-denial, pleasures of love from women, etc. which he has sought all his life are imperfect because they are from outside, not from within himself. This imperfection makes him dissatisfied or unhappy.

Furthermore, Siddhartha becomes happy when he listens to the river because the river reminds him that the outside world is always imperfect. The current of the river is constantly moving at all times, as Siddhartha never stays still. Siddhartha himself has constantly been changing from the day he was born until the moment he stands by the river. His body has changed from young to old. His thinking and perception have also changed. His family has changed. His friendship has changed. His love for Kamala has changed. Kamala herself has also changed from a beautiful young person to an aging woman. Everything in the outside world is always changing like the water current of the river. It is the fact of life. Therefore, we cannot cling to anything from the outside world for happiness, because things from outside are impermanent.

Finally, we can see that wealthy, popular, knowledgeable people are not completely living in happiness. The people who live in happiness are the ones who realize and accept the change and impermanence of life. If people realize that this body is impermanent, that it will get old, die, and decay one day, then death will not be horrible. It's natural that everyone has to die. Thus, people will not be so unhappy facing death. In the Buddha's time, there was a story about this. A woman brought her dead infant to the Buddha. She mourned and lamented for the death of her child, then she asked the Buddha to save her infant. The Buddha promised to bring it back to life if she could find a pea from a family which had no dead member. She went from house to house but could not find the pea because every family had some dead members, either young or old. She came back and told the Buddha that she could not find the pea. Then, the Buddha told her that everyone has to die one day. Her child could not live forever. Nobody could bring it back to life. The woman awoke after hearing those words. She no longer suffered like before.

Ultimately, literature is nothing but carpentry.
With both you are working with reality,
a material just as hard as wood.
Gabriel Garcia Marquez

Jason Spadaro--2nd Place Text-Based Essay
English 098
Instructor: Meredith Kurz

"The Open Boat": A Symbol for Life

Life is an open boat at sea. This is also the setting in Stephen Crane's "The Open Boat." It contains almost all the elements of fiction such as plot, setting, narration, and more. In this particular story the setting is a metaphor or symbol for life.

In the story, four characters (the cook, the correspondent, the oiler, and the captain) are all adrift in an open boat at sea. The open boat represents life. The sea represents the world we live in and how everyone is affected by different things in this world. Crane starts right out by describing the setting which is the open sea with the horizon up ahead: "The horizon narrowed and widened, and dipped and rose, and at times its edge was jagged with waves that seemed thrust up in points like rocks" (1). The horizon is everything people look ahead to. In life, the horizon means something different to everyone; the future looks different to everybody at different times. The fact that the horizon "narrowed and widened, dipped and rose" symbolizes how the future might not always look the same depending on circumstances.

In the beginning of the story, the four characters find themselves in different situations. The cook "squats in the bottom, and looks with his eyes at the six inches of gunwale which separated him from the ocean" (1). One could say that, on the sea of life, the cook is watching the world go by. The oiler, on the other hand, is described as "steering with one of the two oars in the boat, sometimes raising himself suddenly to keep clear of water that swirled in over the stern" (1). In this world, it is usually a choice between sink or swim with almost everything. At this point, the character would rather swim than sink in order to achieve his goals. Like the oiler, the corespondent does the same thing with the other oar, but he wonders what he is doing there. Life can be like this because of the fact that there are times when people wonder why they are here and what good anything is that they do. There are still others who have hit rock bottom or have been shot down. The captain is like this in the beginning. He is injured and lies in the bow.

The men are constantly bombarded by very large waves as they are on a rough sea. The story describes "a singular disadvantage that lies in the sea is the fact that, after successfully surmounting one wave, you discover that there is another behind it" (2). As previously stated, the sea represents the world we live in; consequently, waves on the sea represent the problems with which we are bombarded in this world, and how, when you tackle one problem, there will always be another one following right after it.

Problems that we experience throughout life, however, have a way of bringing people closer together. The story describes all of the characters as being friends. This is very appropriate considering the desperate setting they are in.

Being in their situation with the rough sea, it is no surprise that there is always a chance of their getting shipwrecked. The author speaks of them as being " apropos of nothing" (5). In other words, Crane is saying that shipwrecks never come at the time you are ready for them. He goes on to say, "If men could only train for them and have them occur when the men had reached pink condition, there would be less drowning at sea" (5). The situations of life are a lot like this. Most of them never come at an appropriate time, nor do they fall when you are ready. Besides that, you can never really train for any situations in life that you come in contact with. Most situations you will have to deal with when they come, without preparation.

You cannot start to interpret life until you have really lived it. Old people are wise in this way because they have lived through life and can interpret it. The men in this story were not particularly prepared for what they were going to face, but, after they faced it, they could interpret it at the end of their adventure: "...the wind brought the sound of the great sea's voice to the men on shore, and they then felt that they could be interpreters" (17).

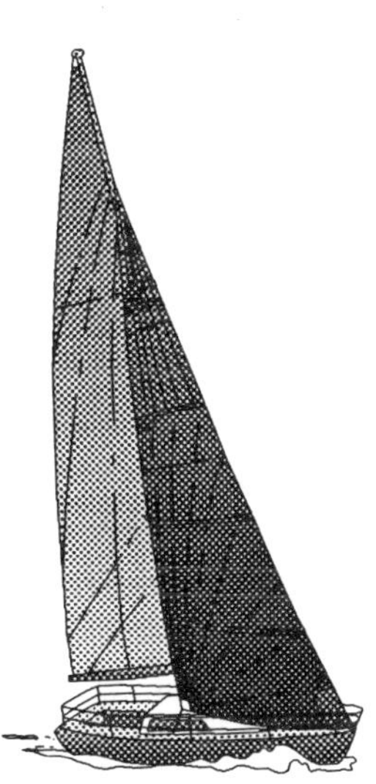

Mary Barmakian--1st Place Text-Based Essay
English 097
Instructor: Eve Caram

Water *Or* Chocolate

How would one choose between stability and lust? Is there the capability inside the soul to deal with such a choice? It seems unfair to be at the point where you must compare the two. It's as though they are as similar as they are different. Like water and chocolate, how can one be given up for the other, why must we decide between them? What the two offer is not comparable, each lacking the goodness which makes the other complete. Throughout the novel, *Like Water for Chocolate,* Tita is torn between two men, each of whom has something extremely different to give her, yet one is just as important as the other. Tita is trapped in the decision between John, who has shown Tita the way to freedom and offers her comfort and security, and Pedro, for whom she has an immense passion and who has allowed her to express her secluded desires.

Tita's relationship with John fluctuates drastically throughout this novel. They begin as friends, almost on a formal basis due to their roles in the lives of the other characters. The reader becomes aware of how strongly Dr. John feels for Tita when he first notices her as a woman: "What a strange sensation he felt when he looked at Tita. A tingling sensation ran through his body, rousing and quickening his sleeping senses. He looked at her as if seeing her for the first time." John is surprisingly charmed by Tita after he sees how beautifully she handles the birth of her nephew. The admiration and respect John has for Tita begins the moment he becomes aware of her strength.

The strong emotional tie that begins between Tita and John happens at a time when Tita needs companionship most. After an incident with her mother, Tita retreats to the dovecote, shutting herself away from the outside world. After spending many hours with her, John is able to bring her down and take her away with him. Tita is then brought to his house where she can feel John's warmth toward her:

> Afterward, John's large loving hands had taken off her clothes and bathed her and carefully removed the pigeon droppings from her body, leaving her clean and sweet-smelling. Finally, he gently brushed her hair and put her in bed with starched sheets.

John cares for her both physically and emotionally. Tita begins to feel an immense amount of gratitude toward John: "Those hands had rescued her from horror and she would never forget it."

Following this gratefulness, Tita has an admiration which she feels toward John. She enjoys watching him work and is left with a sense of peace. An example of her interest in his work is when he is making matches. John tells her how symbolic matches are to the internal flame in the soul and the love you possess. Tita can relate perfectly to all that John talks of and through an unspoken understanding, he becomes aware of the effect his words have on her.

Following this talk and realizing she can love again, Tita wonders if that someone could be John, as she remembers the pleasant sensation that ran through her body when he'd taken her hand.

By giving her space and allowing her the time she needs to heal, John helps Tita grab hold of her freedom and find her real self somewhere beyond the surface. To Tita, John is peace, serenity, and reason. She feels as though she owes him nothing but thanks, for he was the one who had brought her back to her senses. A respectful kind of love has grown inside Tita's heart towards John. He is there for her as a steady support. At times when Tita thinks she will lose it, he is there to offer strength and security:

> They crashed into each other. John held her in his arms just long enough to keep her from freezing. They only touched for a few seconds but it was enough to rekindle her spirit. Tita was beginning to wonder if the feeling of peace and security John gave her wasn't true love.

The love John has for Tita offers her comfort, security, stability and assurance of her true self, whoever she may be. Tita falls into this love for John at a time when she is emotionally unstable. Although that sureness gives Tita the strength that allows her to feel happiness, the overpowering effect of the passion she feels toward Pedro leaves her confused and somewhat incomplete.

Tita has an emotional relationship with Pedro also, though it consists of extremely different sensations. The power between these two is based on desire and yearning. The eternal love that Tita and Pedro share is sparked with a single look:

> That look! She had been walking to the table carrying a tray of egg-yolk candies when she first felt his hot gaze burning her skin. She turned her head, and her eyes met Pedro's. It was then she understood how dough feels when it is plunged into boiling oil. The heat that invaded her body was so real she was afraid she would start to bubble.

Throughout the novel, Laura Esquivel portrays the connection between Tita and Pedro as something entirely sensual. Although Tita's family tradition denies Pedro the ability to love her freely and openly, their longing for each other remains strong until the day they fully come together. It is as though this forbidden love that lingers between them is nourished and strengthened by the fear of discovery that fills their loving with such excitement.

The power of sexual desire is a force that is uncontrollable once it reaches the point where the heart, mind, and soul all covet the same single need. When Tita and Pedro find themselves caught in this lustful aching for one another, their passion is so hot it becomes immortal. Every fiery experience they share leads them to feel overwhelming emotions: "At once their passionate glances fused so perfectly that whoever saw them would have seen but a single look, a single rhythmic and sensual motion, a single trembling breath, a single desire." After allowing him to penetrate her with his eyes, Tita suddenly realizes nothing will be the same. Tita understands, through her own fiery flesh, how fire transforms the elements and how a soul that hasn't been warmed by the fire of love is lifeless.

With all of these amazing feelings, Tita in a sense has given up her soul to Pedro. Although she has an enormous amount of love for John, the difference falls toward the power of desire. Tita needs both kinds of love that John and Pedro offer, but only one can satisfy her deep inside her soul. The overpowering effect she and Pedro have on each other eventually becomes the death of them. Tita dies in the arms of Pedro, experiencing the power of what John made her believe was reason enough to continue to live, and to love. Without John, she may never have been allowed to love Pedro the way she does, when they release the infinite passion that has been contained for so long.

Tita is in the middle of something like water and something like chocolate, needing both in such important but different ways, wondering which part of the soul should be given satisfaction and pleasure. One feeds off of the other in a way that is uncontrollable and unfair. While coming to understand the truth of the matches through Pedro, Tita remembers the words that John had once spoken to her:

> "If a strong emotion suddenly lights all the candles we carry inside ourselves, it creates a brightness that shines far beyond our normal vision and then a splendid tunnel appears that shows us the way that we forgot when we were born and calls us to recover our lost divine origin. The soul longs to return to the place it came from, leaving the body lifeless."

Pedro is Tita's inner fire which allows her to live. Without this chocolate she cannot survive; the passion that feeds the fire will die with him. With the help of John's love, Tita dies in a moment of ecstasy that can only be felt with Pedro.

Which love can you depend on? Something that offers comfort and security, or a love filled with passion and ecstasy? The difference is between what is sensible and what is desired, and the force that drives both sides is powerful. I figure in the end it comes down to your soul and what makes you complete. Emotions are what makes a person who she is, and if those emotions aren't nourished properly, I assume the person cannot be fully alive.

As a woman, I would love to be swept away by passion as powerful as that which Tita and Pedro shared, and at the same time I long for someone someday to love me the way John loved Tita, unconditionally. Is there something in between that will offer complete happiness? How wonderful to experience something that would leave images and memories like those Tita had:

> Images from her first meeting with Pedro in the dark room flooded her mind. The passion with which Pedro had torn away her clothes, causing the flesh beneath her skin to burn beneath the touch of those incandescent hands. The blood simmered in her veins. Her heart burst into a seething passion. Very slowly the frenzy had subsided and given way to infinite tenderness, leaving their shaken souls satisfied.

At the same time, how wonderful it would be to feel the kind of love as accepting and secure as that which was offered to Tita through the words that John spoke:

> "Tita, it doesn't matter to me what you did, there are some things in life that shouldn't be given so much importance, if they don't change what is essential. What you've told me hasn't changed the way I think; I'll say again, I would be delighted to be your companion for the rest of your life but you must think over very carefully whether I am the man for you or not."

I think that anything that perfectly beautiful would be like Water and Chocolate!

Note to students: Page references were not provided in this essay.

Reena Parmar--Honorable Mention
English 098
Instructor: Mary Beth Tegan

M. Butterfly

It is a known fact from our history how different the East and the West are. They have always been considered opposites, but how different are they? From what point are we looking at it? Can the East ever be independent in the eyes of the West or will Westerners always believe they will have power over the East? This is a question that *M. Butterfly* writer, David Hwang, explores through a relationship between a gullible French diplomat and a man playing the role of the submissive "Oriental" woman.

The western man, Gallimard, wants power and believes that if he has an "Oriental" woman, he will have the control. An example given shows stereotypical comments such as, "It's true what they say about oriental girls. They want to be treated bad" (6). He feels as if he can get away with anything he pleases when he says, "The Yankee travels, casting his anchor wherever he wants. Life is not much worth living unless he can win hearts of the fairest maidens" (7). He felt the power when she was begging him in her letters to come see her. Although her shame makes Gallimard realize that "I had finally gained power over a beautiful woman, only to abuse it cruelly" (36). However, this has to be an "Oriental" woman because a western woman would not put up with him.

Gallimard feels threatened by western women because, according to him, western women have gained a lot of personal independence, unlike eastern women. Helga, his wife, does not wait around for her husband to take her out. She is independent and has a life of her own. While she was in China, she was accustomed to going out with her western lady friends to places such as martial arts demonstrations. She would even comment on how good those men looked breaking the thick boards. She felt as if men need not tell her what she could or could not do.

Another example of the western woman's independence is when Gallimard has an extra-extra marital affair with Renee, a student from France. At their first meeting she asks him, "You wanna ... fool around?" (53). Here, the author shows how a western woman can be so independent because she is living in a foreign land. Renee was free to decide on her own.

To compare Song with the two western women, David Hwang shows Song inviting Gallimard up to her apartment for the first time. She says, "I'm a Chinese girl. I've never ... invited a man up to my flat before. The forwardness of my actions makes my skin burn" (31). He shows Song holding on to the values of the past. He displays our misperceptions of how we see Asians. We usually see them with family. Their children and grandparents are always together. We see them as a close knit community. Despite the differences given, Song is also an independent woman. She is living by herself, is making a living on her own, and has lived and had been educated in a foreign land just like Renee. Gallimard feels power when he is with Song. Huang shows the misperceptions we carry as Westerners of how the women in the East are all submissive. They also need power and independence. The author gives Song knowledge of western culture and thinking, which gives her an advantage in misleading Gallimard for twenty years. Gallimard feels powerful and in control, with Song playing his submissive

"Oriental" woman. The other two women did not give him the challenge or even the time of day because of how independent they were.

Just as Gallimard, being a western man, seeks to dominate an "Oriental" woman, western countries also crave power and someone to make them feel as though they really are powerful. For example, Toulon, speaking as a western man and as a western diplomat, says, "Vietnam was our colony" (44). As we see in this example, even the western countries are competing against each other. Just as a man competes for the most beautiful woman, they want the small countries to be the ones they can control.

They also want to take Asian countries under their arms as if they were submissive wives. Two of the myths that Gallimard believes to be true, and tells Toulon, are that "the Orientals simply want to be associated with whoever shows the most strength and power," and that "Orientals will always submit to a greater force" (45-6). Gallimard obviously believes this to be the truth because Song is feeding him with his own misperceptions about the East. It turned out that Gallimard, the new Vice-Consul, was wrong about Vietnam welcoming Americans because they do not stand up to the American fire power. History has shown us the outcome. The western countries experience power when they "colonize" a country. They believe it is now theirs to take care of, which makes them a powerful force. They want to be on a pedestal and recognized for what they are doing. The West wants the East to be as submissive and loyal as their "Oriental" woman.

Looking at Gallimard's situation from our western point of view, we see that our misperceptions about the East blind us. However, looking at the big picture, we can see that the East is just as independent as the West, perhaps not in the same way, but in its own way of running a country, its own families, its own teachings, and its own future. I, as a woman from the East, not the Orient, growing up in the West, see many differences first hand between the two. In a way they are both the same. One wants to conquer and the other will go on without a care, or should I say, carry on without submitting, playing on the misperceptions.

Prose is architecture, not interior decoration....
Ernest Hemingway

Christian Popescu
English 098
Instructor: Sandra Jackson

The Magic of May

Turtle Moon. Two words that let us discover a wonderfully written novel. Alice Hoffman shows the reader passion, tragedy, hatred, magic, and hope, all at the same time, in a piece of literature that makes the reader step into her world of the Turtle Moon. These words also hide a mystery about the fifth month of the year. They are hiding the mystery of May where strange and unexpected things happen.

May, that's exactly the time of the year the story begins. The story takes place in Verity. Verity, a little, insignificant town in the state of Florida and home of more divorced women from New York, than any other town in Florida. One of them is Lucy Rosen who lives in Verity with her son, Keith. Keith is a young boy who can't wait to get away from Verity because of the climate, the school and, tragically, sometimes because of his mother. However, Keith is not the only one hating the hot and very humid weather. Julian Cash, a Verity police officer, also feels miserable under these weather conditions. At the same time a woman gets murdered, leaving a baby--reason enough for Keith to take the baby and to run away. Ignoring the fact that this could make him look like the killer, Keith doesn't give up his dream and fantasy of getting away.

His mother, Lucy, and Julian get together to find them. But at the same time they collide emotionally and experience feelings for each other they never believed to be able to feel, which is almost fatal in the battle to recover Keith and the baby. A battle that almost gets Keith killed by the murderer of the baby's mother. Fortunately, the story takes the right turn and everybody receives what they desire. Keith goes back to his dad in New York, and Lucy starts a new life with Julian in Verity, waiting for the next "Turtle Moon" to come.

Susan Isaacs made a precious comment about Alice Hoffman when she said, "With...her eye for the magic of the mundane, Alice Hoffman seems to know what it means to be a human being." What Isaacs means by this comment is that she thinks Hoffman possesses the talent to express the magic of the "ordinary." A good example of this talent is at the beginning of the third chapter when she writes, "Before there's any light, there is the sound of birds. Their song spirals slowly upward..." (77). Hoffman describes things or situations we never even notice, in such a poetic and romantic way that it is hard to believe how "ordinary" such things have become. With her love for detail she can completely visualize situations for the reader and entirely involve the reader in her magic of the ordinary. A very good example that shows her talent of visualizing moments is when she writes, "The air all around the town limits is so thick that sometimes a soul cannot rise and instead attaches itself to a stranger, landing right between his shoulder blades with a thud that carries no more weight than a hummingbird" (1). You can almost see a soul attaching to a stranger. Her poetic passion enriches her writing with so much power and life that it is hard to believe how beautiful and interesting "ordinary" things can be if you watch them from the right angle.

Connecting her poetic passion for detail to her book, *Turtle Moon*, makes the main themes of this novel seem obvious. By using fairytale elements that include personality changes, tragedies, hatred, magic, and hope, she clearly gives the reader the message to keep feelings alive and to let them navigate their destinies. No matter what, to follow your feelings is one of the most important things in life. Another, no less important, theme of her novel is hope. Without hope, there cannot be life. Without hope there are no dreams and without hope there also are no goals to achieve. These very significant facts make hope a main theme of this novel and of life in general.

Alice Hoffman's main themes in this novel have a very fundamental truth--a fundamental truth that it is essential to be a human being in this world. What she tries to show the reader is that being human is based on having feelings and hope. She shows all these features by letting her characters in *Turtle Moon* be human. A good example is given by Lucy's son, Keith. The boy goes through a lot of inner conflicts. Not being satisfied with his environment, Keith starts rebelling by not going to school and by stealing money from his classmates. A runaway helps him find out more about himself. He realizes the mature side of himself by taking care of the baby he had taken with him. A new friendship with Julian's dog, Arrow, also helps him on his way to the normal Keith. Another example of being human is Julian's discovery of uncontrollable feelings for a person he never noticed and a person he never could have imagined loving. Julian's character shows a dramatic change of personality during *Turtle Moon*. Starting up as a cold, non-talkative person at the beginning of the novel, he ends up being loaded with emotions and feelings towards the end of the novel. These two examples demonstrate to the reader what it means, "being human," in an extraordinary, appealing way.

Also appealing is Hoffman's writing style. Her whole novel is built on hints she gives the reader in the first chapter--intelligently placed hints that make the story more comprehensive later on. To give the novel more life and background information, Alice Hoffman often uses flashbacks. The best example is Julian Cash who always thinks back to when he was young. This is supposed to create a better understanding of Julian's character among the readers. Another tool she uses to make *Turtle Moon* more vivid, is the use of dialogue. By using dialogue, Hoffman makes is easier for readers to identify with the characters involved. Dialogue also awakes the characters to life.

However, the lyrical tool which is the framework of this novel is her descriptions. Alice Hoffman has an exorbitant love for detail. Her talent for subjective writing is amazing. Even boring things Hoffman is able to awake to life through her descriptions.

Seeing this novel as a whole, I find *Turtle Moon* a very valuable piece of literature. Its characters are very human, reflecting feelings and emotions to the fullest. Therefore, the story seems extremely real and full of life. There are also many things that remind me of my life, especially my childhood. I can identify with Keith's character. When I was at his age, I used to do the same things, until I realized that I had to set up some goals I wanted to achieve so that I had something to work for. That's exactly what I am doing now, receiving a higher education so I can have a bright and secure future, no matter whether the Turtle Moon comes or not.

---

*Note to students: For a creative interpretation of **Turtle Moon**, see **The Godfather** in the Creative section.*

Some talked of God, of His mysterious ways,
of the sins of the Jewish people, and their future deliverance.
But I had ceased to pray. How I sympathized with Job!
I didn't deny God's existence but I doubted His absolute justice.
Elie Wiesel, <u>Night</u>

Manuel Marquez
English 098
Instructor: Debby Bogard

The Unescapable Confusion

The book, *Night*, is a true story of a boy's struggles in the German concentration camps during World War II. Through the eyes of the author, Elie Wiesel, we picture some of the worst acts ever committed by man in the history of the human race. Elie, only an adolescent, was a student of the Jewish faith before he began to question the reason for his faith in God, as a result of the pain and suffering that he endures during his experience in the concentration camps. Elie never loses his faith; although there are many times when he says he has. Out of confusion and the sheer will to survive, Elie changes his focus in life from being a student of the Jewish faith to doing and believing anything that could help him survive and stay alive.

Elie studied his prophets through the *Talmud*. The *Talmud* is the Jewish sacred book that says that God is One "...of mercy, sympathy, love, and compassion." Elie did his best to study this sacred book and obey its teachings. He loved his religion. He loved his God. As an early teen he wanted to learn of the teachings of the *Cabbala*, a subject only elder Jews in their thirties were worthy of reading. Elie was approached by an old, poor man named Moshe the Beadle, one day when Elie was in prayer. The old man asked him, "Why do you weep when you pray? Why do you pray?" (2). These questions triggered Elie to question himself further: "Why do I pray? Why did I live? Why did I breathe?" (2). Elie, dumbfounded and confused, could not find an answer. Moshe the Beadle then answered:

> Man raises himself toward God by the questions he asks Him....That is the true dialogue. Man questions God and God answers. But we don't understand His answers. We can't understand them. Because they come from the depths of the soul, and they stay there until your death. You will find the true answers, Eliezer, only within yourself. (2)

Moshe the Beadle then began to teach Elie the *Cabbala* and the teachings of the mystical world. As a result, Elie's knowledge was becoming greater and his faith was becoming stronger.

Moshe the Beadle, along with the other foreign Jews, was evacuated from the city by Hungarian police. Moshe the Beadle later returned with a pale, blank face. He told the remaining Jews what he had witnessed and warned them to leave because the Germans were planning to kill all Jews. He told them how the foreign Jews were ordered to dig their own graves and how babies were thrown in the air and used as targets by the German soldiers. But nobody believed him, not even his own student, Elie. Elie could not see his God, that was so great and compassionate, allowing such inhumanities to occur. The people then looked at Moshe the Beadle as a poor old man who had gone crazy and felt sympathy for him.

It was then Elie's turn to leave. The Germans arrived in his town to evacuate the remaining Jews. Elie was headed to hell. It wasn't too bad at first. The Germans didn't treat them so badly. Then came Auschwitz, and Elie's faith was being taken from him just like his family. After witnessing many horrible deaths, the older, wiser men reassured the younger Jews: "You must never lose faith, even when the sword hangs over your head. That's the teaching of our sages..."(29). Elie saw men as well as children walk into a crematory and come out as a gray cloud of smoke. He was now confused. How could such a compassionate God allow these horrible acts to be committed? That night when the Jewish men were reciting the Kaddish, the prayer for the dead, Elie spoke of his confusion: "For the first time, I felt revolt rise up in me. Why should I bless His name? The Eternal, Lord of the Universe, the All-Powerful and terrible, was silent. What had I to thank Him for?" (31). Elie is now questioning his faith and his belief in God.

Elie was beginning to lose faith. He talks about the death of his God:

> Never shall I forget those flames that consumed my faith forever. Never shall I forget the nocturnal silence which deprived me, for all eternity, of all desire to live. Never shall I forget those moments which murdered my God and my soul and turned my dreams into dust. Never shall I forget these things, even if I am condemned to live as long as God Himself. Never. (32)

This statement proves that he is experiencing some confusion because he first talks about his God and faith being dead forever, but later he says he will never forget what he has seen even if he lives as long as God himself. Elie later says, "The student of the *Talmud*, the child that I was, had been consumed in the flames. There remained only a shape that looked like me. A dark flame had entered my soul and devoured it" (34). Then, without thinking, he talks of God again in a positive way: "I thanked God in an improvised prayer, for having created mud in His infinite and wonderful universe" (35). His faith in God is still there. He just has to find something to be thankful for. Here he was thanking God for creating mud that covered his new shoes so that the soldiers could not see they were new and take them away. But he really doesn't have much to be thankful for, so as a result his faith comes and goes.

One evening while Elie was in bed, he talked about his feelings towards God: "Some talked of God, of His mysterious ways, of the sins of the Jewish people, and of their future deliverance. But I had ceased to pray. How I sympathized with Job! I did not deny God's existence, but I doubted His absolute justice" (42). Elie once again is tempted to forget God. He understands how Job felt when God took everything he had and made his life a living hell. God had now done the same to him. Through all the starvation, pain and suffering, Elie still found occasions to thank God. Unfortunately, this wasn't very often. Most of his conversations with God were out of anger and questioning. When they witness the young boy hanging from a rope, suffering his slow death, many Jews began to lose their faith. "Where is God now?" (62), asked a man behind Elie as they walked by the hanging bodies. Elie internally replied, "Where is He? Here He is--He is hanging here on this gallows..." (62). Again Elie is upset with God for allowing the Germans to commit such a horrible act.

With all that Elie had been through, he exploded unto God:

> What are You, my God, compared to this afflicted crowd, proclaiming to You their faith, their anger, their revolt? What does your greatness mean, Lord of the

universe, in the face of all this weakness, this decomposition, and this decay?

Why do You still trouble their sick minds, their crippled bodies? (63)

Elie had seen enough. He had read of his God of sympathy, God of love, and compassion. But where was His sympathy and love now? Elie wanted to see something good happen for a change, something positive. He wanted to see a sign to show him that his God still existed.

Upon arriving in Auschwitz, the prisoner in charge gave a few words vital for their survival: "Have faith in life. Above all else, have faith. Drive out despair, and you will keep death away from yourselves" (38). This was true. This is why Elie was able to survive. Without faith they would have given up and surrendered their lives to the Germans. Although he didn't know it, it was his faith that was keeping him alive. It is easy for one to say that being put in his situation, one would never lose faith in God. But imagining it and living through are not the same. Elie lived through it. In confusion, and in faith, he survived.

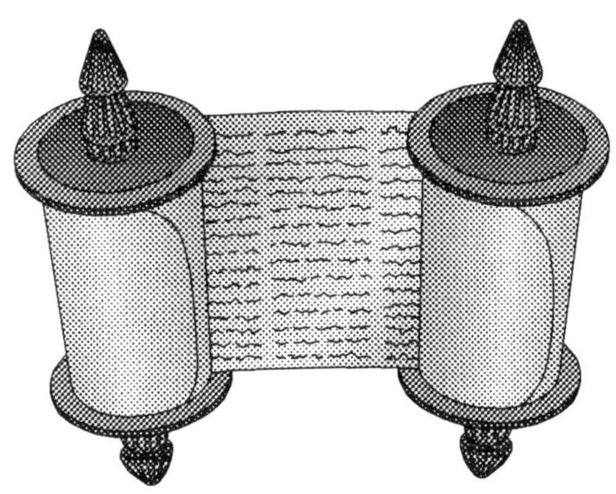

A conviction grew in me that Moshe the Beadle
would draw me with him into eternity, into that time
where question and answer would become one.
Elie Wiesel, <u>Night</u>

Yuria Takehana
English 098
Instructor: Debby Bogard

The Lost Faith

When people face a crisis, they usually turn to religion. It is said that a savior religion gets stronger when a society is out of control. Apuleius, who lived through the mid-decades of the second century A.D., and was born in North Africa, wrote about what would happen when the gap widened between reality and the minds of men. He suggested that people turn to a Goddess (he believed in the Isis cult) so that they would be saved. However, if something happens to those who already have a strong faith in God, what do they do? Do they turn away from their faith?

Eliezer Wiesel is a witness and a victim of the Holocaust, the genocide of Jews by the Nazis, in Germany. His book, *Night*, was written after a long silence. What made him finally write about what had happened to him?

He begins his book with his peaceful childhood memory. The word "peaceful" can best describe his childhood because he was seeking God. It might not have been very peaceful when he was struggling to find a master to guide him. But when he met Moshe the Beadle, he knew that a conviction grew in him. Then, his master was sent to one of the concentration camps, and he managed to escape. When he got back and told the town's people about the Holocaust, nobody believed him. Eliezer could see his changes: there was no longer any joy in his eyes. "He no longer sang. He no longer talked to me of God" (4). However, Eliezer couldn't understand Moshe the Beadle at that time, even though Eliezer's destiny was to follow Moshe the Beadle's experience.

The time came for Eliezer's family to be sent to Auschwitz. Despite his faith, his doubt started to grow when he saw people who might be from his own family being thrown into the fire: "Never shall I forget those flames which consumed my faith forever" (32). The prisoners could do nothing but weep. His father, whom Eliezer had never imagined capable of tears, was weeping and praying in vain. Eliezer asked questions to himself: "Why should I bless His name? The Eternal, Lord of the Universe, the All-Powerful and Terrible was silent. What had I to thank Him for?" (31). Despite Moshe the Beadle's words, questions and answers never became one.

Eliezer faced death on the first day in Auschwitz, and his faith was already gone into the fire. Prayer came out of his mouth in spite of himself, but it wasn't his will. His pure soul which could believe in God was destroyed: "I too had become a completely different person....A dark flame had entered into my soul and devoured it" (34). A prayer became nothing but just a word.

On the eve of Rosh Hashanah, the last day of the Jewish year, thousands of voices repeated the benediction. Eliezer kept asking himself, while listening to others praying: "Why should I bless Him?" Eliezer blamed God for all the things which had happened to the Jews:

"...these men here, whom You have betrayed, whom You have allowed to be tortured, butchered, gassed, burned, what do they do? They pray before You! They praise Your name!" (64). Eliezer noticed that the prayer kept stopping every moment "as though he did not have the strength to find the meaning beneath the words" (64). Eliezer did not deny God's existence, therefore he could accuse Him of His silence: "I no longer accepted God's silence" (66).

On the selection days when weak people were chosen to be sent to the crematory, more people lost their faith. Akiba Drumer, a fellow prisoner, once said, "God is testing us. He wants to find out whether he can dominate our base instincts and kill the Satan within us" (49). But later, even Akiba Drumer lost his faith: "Poor Akiba Drumer, if he could have gone on believing in God, he would not have been taken by the selection. But as soon as he felt the first cracks forming in his faith, he had lost his reason for struggling and had begun to die" (73). A rabbi who had always prayed said to Eliezer, "It's the end. God is no longer with us" (73). People who once had strong faith in God were feeling abandoned by God.

How could a 15 year-old boy possibly keep his faith when he was surrounded by those who had lost theirs? After the selection days, he didn't mention God except once, when he saw the son of Rabbi Eliahou leaving his father: "In spite of myself, a prayer rose in my heart, to that God in whom I no longer believed. Give me strength never to do what Rabbi Eliahou's son has done" (87). But the dead were left without being given any prayer nor a tear. Nobody could see any hope, only the endless darkness. Eliezer lost his father just before the prisoners were free. His father, who had gone through all the agony with his son, finally left his son for the eternal rest. Eliezer was realizing that he was doing the same thing as Rabbi Eliahou's son had done, despite his prayer. God remained silent, even to Eliezer's last wish. No prayer was given over his dead father, nor tears: "I did not weep, and it pained me that I could not weep. But I had no more tears. And, in the depths of my being, in the recesses of my weakened conscience, could I have searched it, I might perhaps have found something like--free at last!" (106).

When they were finally free, they thought about nothing but bread. No dignity was left. Eliezer looked at himself in a mirror for the first time since the ghetto: "From the depths of the mirror, a corpse gazed back at me. The look in his eyes, as they stared into mine, has never left me" (109). He is still trapped in his memory, at the time when he thought that God wasn't with him. He would be free when he got his faith back. He started to write in order to take the first step to get his faith back.

Persuasive
Essays

Geobert Abboud
English 098
Instructor: Debby Bogard

Misconstrued

So, what's so new about sex?

I don't know- what is so new about sex?

Imagination.

Imagination?

What? Forget it...this is stupid. Where are you from?

It's not where I'm from...it's where I've been and where I'm going that matters. How about you?

You're pretty damn quick with words...tell me something about yourself.

Creativity is my business. It is my job to herd the cattle, lead the horses to the water, and then make them do just about anything the client wants.

I seem to understand a bit. Interesting.

So how old are you anyway?

Seventeen. And yourself?

I'll certainly never see seventeen again. I was there about thirteen years ago. So, are you doing research specifically about sex, the flexibility of the human body, or just trying to get some pointers?

Well, I just like learning about it and its effects on human relationships...and whether or not sex is necessary to maintain a certain relationship between two people.

Explain "certain relationship."

You know...is it necessary that a boyfriend/girlfriend relationship be maintained through sex...that is, is sex needed to show you love a girlfriend?

No. It's not. Take some priceless advice: be a friend first. If you love them for who they are and not what they give, you'll save yourself about four years of bad experiences with women.

And not to mention you'll end up with someone you truly love for the right reasons. Then the sexual part of the relationship will be more fulfilling than anything you can imagine.

I'll be sure to keep that in mind.

That's not to say that I believe you have to wait until you're married, just wait for the right person.

But, wouldn't you marry the right person?

Not necessarily. I mean, not if you don't believe in marriage.

I don't really understand. Marriage is a step further in a relationship. I think it is one of the last steps. Marriage is commitment, and if you don't have commitment, you'll never find the right person. Just make sure it's someone who's your best friend, your lover, and your soul mate. Never consider it for any other reasons than those.

Yes...I believe you're right. It sounds as though you have a personal dilemma with someone in your life.

Kinda....I mean, not about marriage. I have another question...what's a friend?

My perspective is that there really are no friends. Just situational acquaintances. Your life is a book and everyone you meet is words on a page in a chapter of that book. As you move through life you'll begin to see this pattern. You'll meet people and they and you move on to other parts or chapters of your life. As far as those acquaintances, though, you should look for honesty, and of course, chemistry.

Hold up...if they are just situational acquaintances, then the one you marry is just an acquaintance? I think not...the one you marry should be your friend and therefore friends do exist. I mean to say that I don't want my lover to be just a word in a book. I want my lover to be the whole damn book!

I can do nothing but agree with you.

You probably don't have too many problems, huh?

We all have problems. The difference is how we choose to deal with them. If you don't play chess, you should learn. The strategy behind chess comes in handy with life situations. And by the way, you sound like you're a pretty smart guy with a good head on your shoulders.

Thanks...I play chess...but I'm not that great. How did you attain such a wonderful knowledgeable mind? How did you learn of your methods to deal with problems?

I've learned more in my life by watching other people make mistakes. If you pay attention to what goes on around you, you begin to realize where not to go in life and what paths are the better ones. Pay close attention to people and what makes them tick. Find out what their "hot buttons" are. When you learn to do this you'll see that people really are in groups of behavior patterns, and then you can begin to predict their motions. I learned by doing--that is, I learned through experience and remembering as I went along.

Experience through others? Pretty cool...I guess I gotta live a little longer to learn more...

We all learn as we go along. We never stop learning. But if you understand now what to look for and what to store, you'll be so far ahead in the world. Sometimes I think I'm just an old soul that has lived here before. My life has moved very quickly. I'm a very young executive in my business. And I credit much of that to what I've just shared with you. Life can be great if you know how to handle it.

Thank you very much for having had this conversation with me.

I'm glad that I can be of some help in sharing my thoughts.

Thanks again.

Oh... and one last thing before I go. Commitment is believing in the person you're with and trusting them enough to be with them and share with them your life. But also understand that we are all humans. And sometimes if a situation doesn't work, it's only right to be honest with one another and go on with separate lives. Goodnight...it's been great.

Wait! "Separate lives?" How can that be possible? Shouldn't commitments last for a long time? Maybe for life? If they didn't, they'd be worthless...right?

Yes, I suppose.

Well, until next time.

Until next time....

One may certainly notice how an individual's mind can be affected by the thoughts and teachings of others, just as I have, through this conversation with a woman on America Online. Society is constructing a barrier around each one of us, disabling us from understanding an extremely important necessity of life--friendship. This relationship is indeed deteriorating.

Primarily, I must discuss ethics and morality, both of which deal with the principles of right and wrong, for these two philosophical terms are the dawning of friendship. Ethics is primarily concerned with attempting to define what is good or bad for the individual and for society. As Compton's Encyclopedia defines it, Ethics is the "branch of philosophy concerned with human behavior, morality, and responsibilities of people to each other and to society." In any case, one must ask oneself whether or not one must be "good" at all times, or "good" depending on the situation in which one finds oneself. In dealing with friendship, one must treat another with kindness, respect, love and care. Therefore, no friendship can possibly relate to anything immoral. Many philosophers, past and present, have said that "we, as humans, do not willingly do what is bad for us but may do what is bad for others if it appears that good for us will result" (Compton's). This ill-doing is not the beginning of friendship but rather the start of hostile actions performed between two groups or individuals.

Next, I must further my discussion of friendship as an ontological possibility. Aristotle created the term "practical wisdom." He called it "practical" since it dealt with being "inclined to action, both on the part of the individual and on the part of society." It had to do with what should or should not be done. Who is to say who are to be friends (i.e. "like seeks like" or "two of a trade never agree")? Friendship has nothing to do with materialism; therefore, it has to be more ideal. Friendship, not only between two people, but also among groups, should deal with the idea of "utilitarianism," that "social actions are valid if they promote the greatest good for the greatest number" (Compton's). Friendship must consist of love and care, meaning that one must give without expecting a reciprocation of one's generosity.

I have come to realize that friendship will soon die out since people are confusing "desires" with "strong affections." Although we know a difference exists between "like" and "love," we do not understand it. This is where we must distinguish between friends and acquaintances. No one can have a friendship based on need, "...nor can people admit one another to friendship, or be friends at all, until each has been proved lovable and trustworthy to the other" (Aristotle). People must decide what is good for others as well as for themselves. That is, they should expect that good for them applies equally to other people. "To be able to treat others in the same way one treats oneself," Aristotle said, "it is necessary to have the three virtues of practical wisdom: temperance, courage, and justice" (Compton's). Aristotle further wrote that "friendship seems to consist rather in loving than in being loved; hence, where love is found in due proportion, people are permanent friends, and their friendship is permanent."

There may be different types of friendships (i.e. brothers, father/son, husband/wife, etc.). And though they may be very different, there is always one common factor--it is the given love between the people that creates the friendship and makes it last for a long period of time.

Works Cited

Aristotle.   *L'Ethique a Nicomaque.* R.A. Gauthier and J.Y. Jolif, eds., 3 vols.
     Louvain, 1958.
Compton's Encyclopedia. Online. *(Incomplete)*

Note to students: Refer to your handbook for the correct method of citing online sources.

After all, the ultimate goal of all research
is not objectivity, but truth.
Helene Deutsch

Javier Pina--Honorable Mention

English 098
Instructor: Sandra Jackson

Is the DARE Program Effective at the Elementary Level?

In the past few years drugs have been a major problem among people of all ages. Recently, this problem has increased among adolescents and children. Various types of drug resistance programs have been implemented in schools. These programs aim at teaching adolescents and children how to resist peer pressure. One of these programs is the Drug Abuse Resistance Education program, also known as DARE. "DARE is usually classified as a program offering peer resistance techniques and providing social influence" (Clayton et al., 1991). This program is being offered in elementary schools throughout California as well as in other states. I ask, does this program really work? According to researcher Michele A. Harmon, 341 students who took part in the DARE program showed no difference in frequency in the use of cigarettes, marijuana, coping strategies, rebellious behavior and self-esteem (1993). For this and many other reasons, the DARE program should be removed from the California elementary school system.

Authors of "How Effective is Drug Abuse Resistance Education?: A Meta-analysis of project DARE Outcome Evaluations" (Susan Ennett et al., 1994), argue that DARE is effective in reducing the use of drugs, but only temporarily. Several studies of the effectiveness of the DARE program have been conducted on 5th graders. Follow-ups have been done among this same group of people after a two-year period, and have found that the effectiveness, if any, had vanished.

Susan Ennett and Dennis P. Rosenbaum, also researchers, did a two-year follow-up on 1,334 adolescents who participated in the DARE program, and found that the program had no effect on their peer resistant skills (1994), which is the program's goal. If this is the case, we see that this program is not working. Teachers and students are wasting educational time during this program which is not effective. Instead of wasting time trying to teach our children concepts which are too sophisticated at their level, they should be taught those lessons in math and English which are not only going to be at their level of understanding, but will also be beneficial to them for the rest of their lives.

In addition, DARE also wastes tax money. The majority of US workers support this program involuntarily by having taxes deducted from their pay checks. What's the point of wasting thousands of tax dollars on a program that teaches children resistance skills, when these skills will have disappeared by the time these children get to high school, which is where peer pressure is most prevalent?

While DARE aims at teaching peer resistance skills, many children have gotten something completely different out of this program. For many children, "DARE has made a positive impact on awareness of the costs of using alcohol and cigarettes, and perceptions of the media's portrayal of these substances" (Ennett et al., 1991). Is this what we want our children to learn in the fifth grade? Is it right to waste time in the classroom and tax money so that children can learn that a box of cigarettes costs $2.25? Is knowing the cost of a box of cigarettes going to help them to resist peer pressure in high school, or is it going to let them know how much money to obtain to be able to purchase cigarettes and other substances? A possible explanation for the lack of effectiveness of the DARE program is that the fifth-grade mind is not mature enough to absorb the concept of peer pressure.

If the fifth-grade mind is not capable of absorbing resistance skills from the DARE program, then a better solution would be to delay this program for middle school, since substance abuse in the fifth grade is rare (Becker et al., 1992). During middle school, students will be on the verge of being in contact in some way with drug use, so the program might be more effective during this time.

Thus, we have seen that the DARE program is not effective at an elementary school level. Since the effectiveness is temporary and fifth-grade students are too young to understand the concept of the program, then implementing this program at levels right before high school might be a better idea. The year just before high school and the first year of high school are the years when drugs are not only the easiest to obtain but also when the peak of curiosity rises. I, as a previous participant, agree with the researchers' findings. If this program was effective, I, as well as many other participants of the DARE program, would never have tried any type of drug. Therefore, school administrators must consider the effectiveness of the program and the waste of educational time (Becker et al., 1992).

---

*References

Becker, Harold K., Agopian, Michael W., & Yeh, Sandy. (1992). Impact evaluation of drug abuse resistance education (DARE). *Journal of Drug Education, 22.*

Clayton, Richard R., Cattarello, Anne, & Walden, Katherine P. Sensation seeking as a potential mediating variable for school-based prevention intervention: A two-year follow-up of DARE. Special Issue: Communication and drug abuse prevention. *Health Communication, 3.*

Ennett, Susan T., Tobler, Nancy S., Ringwald, Christopher L., & Flewelling, Robert L. (1994). How effective is drug abuse resistance education?: A meta-analysis of Project DARE outcome evaluations. *American Journal of Public Health, 84.*

Harmon, Michele A. (1993). Reducing the risk of drug involvement among early adolescents: An evaluation of Drug Abuse Resistance Education (DARE). *Evaluation Review, 17.*

Note for students: Sample of APA format. Page numbers are missing and would follow volume numbers and (issue) numbers. See your handbook for accuracy.

*Writing saved me from the sin
and inconvenience of violence.*
Alice Walker

Cedrick Holmes--2nd Place Persuasive Essay

English 098
Instructor: Edna Burow

If You Don't Live Where I Live, You Can't See What I See

Tipper Gore, the wife of Vice President Al Gore, wrote what she thought about the rap industry in the essay "Hate, Rape, and Rap." Some of the things she wrote I agree with, but there are a few things that I have to disagree with. I don't know where the Second Lady lived when she was my age, but I can almost guarantee that she hasn't seen the things that I have. I have seen a man die, and I have experienced things that some people would have had a heart attack from. Situations such as being robbed at gun point and seeing my mother snatched out of her bed by a gun-toting maniac, have inspired me to write lyrics to raps of my own. I write what I feel because it's my best work. Ice T isn't speaking about anything that youth living in the ghetto don't know about already. We see so much and don't realize how bad things are until we get older, and wiser. Rap is a way to get the pain out of our systems, and get paid to do it. Can you blame us for being real? If you think you can, it's because you don't understand what we go through.

I'll freely admit that some rappers go too far with some of the things that they say, but I also believe that they do it because the rules allow them to. America is definitely the land of free speech, so why are the people who enforce the rules, trying to change the rules? Because we found a way to use it to an advantage? Do the rules change every time America thinks they aren't right? If so, America is acting like a big kid, getting all of the penalties he calls, simply because it's his ball.

Writing after a tragic experience helps ease the pain of remembering what happened. I wrote a rap called "S.C. Story" (South Central Story) after seeing a man die in my driveway. The lyrics are as follows:

11:45 still up,
got to roll to the 0, time to go
just when I hear a buck.
My first reaction was to duck,
Wanna know what's up, so I truck unto the window, uh
It was a child of the dead
In a puddle was spread, all that red, because of poison lead
and then I thought how could this be?
He had fell to the streets, oh why me to be the first to see?
Unto the 911,
but this nigga was done, there none in time to save this one.
I seen him take his last breath,

it was a run in with death, what was next, the sheets and stains were left
and so they scrubbed until it hurt,
uh, yes, they spread it, and spread it, poison lead is what had made it worse.
But now I'm back into the glory,
just sit back and relax, this is a S.C. Story, Yeah.

My lyrics were not as vulgar as some of today's rappers', but in the body and the chorus, I said the word "nigga" a few times. I have gotten mixed reactions from people who have listened to the song. Some people think I should stop saying "nigga" and some feel that the song wouldn't be right without it.

I will agree with Mrs. Gore when she attacks the racism in music. Things like that are simply uncalled for. Racism is in no way comparable to singing about what people have seen and experienced. If racism is experienced first hand, that's another story. I don't feel anyone has the right to degrade another race on records and tapes. That is hate and hate has to be taught. Killing in the ghetto has been going on for a long time and won't stop because of that reason. Things such as money shortages and greed contribute to the violence of the streets. Hate can be stopped in the home at an early age. I watched a show just today that featured "KKK Moms." That was a perfect example of how hate starts and why it is kept throughout a person's life. What our parents teach us affects us like nothing else in the world. Some of things they say will affect us from the time that they say it until we die.

I'm almost sure that Mrs. Gore doesn't listen to rap. I'm in no way stereotyping her, but I think she only notices the bad in it. She in no way gives examples of how rap should be, nor the positive things she notices about it now. It's not right to criticize a whole industry without looking at the good. It's also not right to blame increases in crime on rap, without mentioning other things that might have caused the increase. Let's argue using logic. Then maybe we might get somewhere.

Works Consulted

Gore, Tipper. "Hate, Rape, and Rap." *Models for Writers*. Eds. Alfred Rosa,
    and Paul Escholz. New York: St. Martin's Press, 1995.

The writings of the day show the quality of
the people as no historical reconstruction can.
Edith Hamilton

Nektar Toukhladjian
English 098
Instructor: Anne Kellenberger

Sexism in the Nineties

"Our culture has always smacked girls on the head when they moved into a broader culture that is rife with girl-hurting 'isms,' such as sexism and lookism, which is the evaluation of a person solely on the bases of appearance." This is a sentence taken out of my favorite book called *Reviving Ophelia* written by Mary Phypher, Ph.D. It is about adolescent girls facing the everyday dangers of being young and female. By reading this book I realized how hard it is to be a woman in a society where everyone expects you to be perfect looking and perform roles that demonstrate a false self.

Sexism has always been part of our culture. Most women don't seem to care about this, but I do. I care because I was brainwashed for many years to believe in male dominance. I was raised in an environment where all the actions were governed by males. Until a few months ago, I never paid attention to what was going on around me. For a long time I was asleep but when I woke up I discovered a completely different world. I saw females worrying more about their looks than education. I saw women not pursuing their goals because of their families' old-fashioned beliefs. I also met some adolescent girls using drugs and alcohol to escape from the harsh realities of life. All of these findings made me realize that too much is expected from women and they are just unable to cry out for help.

Should girls act in certain ways to get attention? Is it wrong for them to be smart and not good looking? Are females judged by their looks or expression of opinions? These questions often confuse girls so they begin to lose their true selves to meet the expectations of the environment surrounding them. Girls are often expected to look nice, act stupid, and be inferior to boys. It angers me when I see women not achieving their goals because of outside influences. Just a few days ago I heard that my fifteen-year-old cousin is getting engaged to be married. I am kind of happy for her but I am also sad because after having a family she'll be unable to go to college and get educated. Later on, her husband will use her lack of education against her. In my opinion, it's all her parents' fault because they taught her that having a family is more important than a career. Don't get me wrong. I believe in strong family values but I also believe that everyone has a right to expand their knowledge enough to have a decent job. It is wrong for women to be at home fulfilling devalued house-hold duties and expecting men to support them,

Some people would like to think that now women have lots of rights, but believe me, sexism still exists. For example, we could compare the girls attending elementary and junior high schools. In elementary schools girls are as active as the boys, but how come in junior high schools most of them become depressed and lose self-esteem? The answer is very simple. In their early adolescent years girls learn to follow certain rules, but if some of them refuse to go along, society begins to treat them rudely. That's why girls isolate themselves in their own world and get depressed. In the 1990's, girls experience a more complicated life. They are expected to forget their childish activities and act as attractive as possible to win attention from boys. Most girls are even discouraged to perform well in classes because boys prefer women who are logically inferior to them. When I was going to high school, my way of getting attention from boys was helping them cheat. I tried to fit in by letting them copy from my papers and get good grades. Some of them thanked me but most of them tried to keep their distance because I was too smart to be seen with them. Unfortunately, I began to change to meet the expectations. First of all, I changed my appearance. I bought expensive clothes and I had plastic surgery to get rid of my traditional nose. My grades started dropping and I noticed people paying attention to me. They actually asked me to be in their groups. That was all a girl, with low self-esteem like me, needed. These types of examples are common in every culture but to a different extent. The old-fashioned stereotypes of women traditionally pass from one generation to another but they never completely disappear.

Some stereotypes also include the idea that women are not good at math and science-related subjects so girls know from the start that they are not expected to get good grades in those classes. Most of the time girls concentrate on home economics and English. Another old-fashioned stereotype is that women are good at assistant types of jobs like nurses or secretaries. Even some members of my family think that this is true and it scares me. For example, my aunt thinks that I should keep on working as a medical assistant in a doctor's office and quit college. She said that I shouldn't think of continuing my education in a university because in the future my husband will support me and it isn't nice for a woman to get paid more than a man: "Woman's money in not eatable," she said. It means that when the man makes money it's used for the family, but the woman's money is easy come and easy go. I don't think that's necessarily true because there are so many families that I know who depend on a woman's paycheck, and I don't think that their money is unwisely spent. The most important fact about these families is that the women are not secretaries but graduates of universities.

There is a way to face this problem of sexism. First of all, our society's old-fashioned beliefs must change. We should all view males and females as equals. We also should teach new rules to the upcoming generation of girls and encourage them to do well in schools for a bright future. Girls must learn to act and look natural. They should know that looks don't mean anything as long as they are smart, and being smart is a beauty in itself.

Xuan Chung
English 098
Instructor: Sharon Maselli

The Sad Truth

China has a rich culture and an amazing past, from the Great Wall to its Industrial Revolution. China is a place of wealth, not only because of its fine gold or Chinese silk, but because of its culture and its undying roots. Yet, sometimes I am ashamed of my Chinese culture because it discriminates against women. I am angered because most of its past excludes women. When I think of women's great effect on our society, I cannot believe that we were considered useless and a waste of food.

Chinese females were treated like dirt, or more accurately just like cows, which, when grown big, can be sold to someone for money. Because the boys carry the family name, they were like gold to their parents while the girls were like leeches. So in many families, girls didn't have the right to do anything, except all the chores, but they were still considered useless. Sometimes they were sold by their parents at birth to other families to be brides, who also did the most work in their in-laws households.

In the Chinese culture, women were treated badly. During the eras of the past, they were like ornaments hung on their men, to decorate and serve their husbands. Men could have as many mates as they wanted just as long as they could afford them. But if a woman was caught with more than one man, she was put in a human-sized basket filled with rocks and thrown into the river, left to drown. As for the man, he just had to say it was the woman's fault, that she had seduced him, and he was a free man. Even today in China and the United States, Chinese girls are treated poorly. If a teenage girl and a boy have sex, and she tells someone, she'll be shamed and called nasty names. But if the boy tells, he will soon become an idol to his peers. A girl still has a lot to lose, either way.

I remember at the tender age of ten, my grandma, Chue, told me very horrible stories to remind me how lucky I am and how grateful I should be in this free country. I didn't dare believe these true stories. My grandmother was married twice and the first marriage was an arranged marriage. My grandmother was starved, beaten up, and disowned by her own mother when she gave birth to the third girl for her husband. I was more horrified when she explained to me that she was lucky that they didn't strangle the baby. In the 1930's, the days of my grandmother's teen life, almost everybody killed their baby girls or left them in the streets where cats, dogs, or rats were fed.

When my grandmother's first husband died, she became a widow for a few years. My grandmother chopped wood, worked in a factory making bowls, and had little or no time to care for her daughters. It was hard during that time; she was alone with her daughters and often

hungry. They didn't have much to eat because wages doing different tasks weren't enough.
They ate very watery porridge, often only with little pieces of pickled vegetables. My
grandmother was forced to find herself another husband, but fortunately she found someone this
time who was nice to her. She got married and had my mother, Chan Tu Hoang. Back in those
days in China, women weren't suppose to marry twice: "Once a widow, always a widow." My
grandmother was considered dirty to her first in-laws; they didn't understand the hardships she
had to go through and were really mean to her. They despised my grandmother and my mother,
who became the gossip of their little village.

I realized many things as my grandmother told me these stories. My grandmother is a
strong person within. She has gone through a lot and life has not been exactly treating her
kindly, but she takes it as a part of her life with no complaints. She is a survivor of
discrimination. One thing we can learn from my grandmother is that we are all strong inside and
there are many ways we can use this strength. Women are just as good as men in many ways,
sometimes even better. All this has happened to us women because discrimination was part of
our culture, and a sad part. We were raised to believe that we were just simply not good enough.
All our lives we were taught to be loyal servants to our husbands and that without them we could
not stand on our own. Now we should stand up together and stand strong, to defend what has
been lost, to defend our ground.

I came to America on September 9,1979, with my grandmother Chue, my parents Chan
and Phu Chung, my older sister Anh and my older brother Quoang. Although Anh, Quoang and
I were born in Saigon, Vietnam, we are Chinese. My parents' dreams were young and hopeful.
They've escaped their country, Vietnam, seeking the American Dream. My family first arrived
at Santa Ana, California, seeking equal opportunity and freedom.

I am fortunate to have my life here, in America, the land of opportunities. I was raised to
achieve all my goals and have only the best for myself. I am angered that injustice is happening
everywhere. Now and a long time ago.

My dad was always by my side. I realized that when my dad once told me that I could
make a difference. He said, "I know many Chinese people look down on girls and think they are
useless, but I always thought differently... I love you the most out of our family not only because
you are my daughter, but because my faith lies with you."

All books are either dreams or swords.
You can cut, or you can drug, with words.
Amy Lowell

Arat Apik
English 098
Instructor: Anne Kellenberger

Why Hate?

Racism--the sick ideology which caused most of the trouble in the twentieth century. The ideology that we thought died after WW II has risen again in these last two decades. Why is this ideology receiving widespread support again, after the dark years of the early twentieth century? Why are racist panics increasing in Europe? Does it have something to do with the global economic recession that we are experiencing now, like the one we had in the first four decades of this century? What causes a person to be biased against another group? Do all racists have the same character type or they are different?

First, if one is determined to hate another nation or ethnic group, one won't have too much trouble finding excuses. Naturally there are some cultural differences between nations but these differences should not give a priority to one nation over another. However, a racist thinks that whatever s/he owns (color, language, religion) is better than those s/he hates. If one gets on the highway of hatred there is no stop. First one hates one group for something, then another for another reason, and so on. After a while one starts to feel alone in the world and starts to believe that one deserves everything that is available, especially the things that belong to the group one hates. "Who cares? It belongs to them? They are not human. They should be erased, and perish from the face of the world, for the sake of civilization." The person I tried to picture above is an extreme example, I know, but these kinds of people are not extinct. They are still living and killing.

While reading history books, I discovered a group and called them "Moderate Racists." These people never admit that they are racists. These people wouldn't burn a cross or a church, but they would have no reaction if somebody else did it. History proves that aggression against a minority becomes fatal when intentionally approved by "Moderate Racists," who represent the largest portion of a society. These people support the crimes with their silence. Their lack of response makes the killers think that they will never be punished for what they are doing. What makes these people moderate racists? Their reasons are usually different from the ones of extreme racists. They usually discriminate against other races or minorities for economic reasons. These people are usually from the middle class and they are concerned about their jobs. This is exactly the case in Europe now. The latest polls show that the racist party of LePen in France raised its votes to about eleven percent, and in Germany Neo-Nazis started to kill again. Both are against immigrants because they are taking the jobs that could have possibly been given to the real citizens of the country. By using this strategy, they started to gain more and more support, and this will continue if nobody does anything. Moderate Racists are pleased because the more radical racists are scaring the hell out of immigrants and causing newcomers to think twice. The same mistakes that were made before WW I and WW II are being repeated in Europe. Racists are pleased.

Racism is especially dangerous when it is directed to the minorities of a country. Because these minorities are not citizens, they can't protect themselves. They don't have armed forces to protect them or to scare the murderers. The aggressive movements against minorities usually result in huge numbers of people being killed, such as what happened to the Armenians and Jews during the early part of this century. Minorities had nothing or no one to protect them and the murderers chose the best times to commit their crimes, during the First and Second World Wars. Both Turkey and Germany were in economic crises at that particular time, and each country's government blamed its minorities for the situation: "They (the target ethnic group) are doing all the jobs and controlling the economy of the country. The only reason for the economic recession and poverty is them because they don't give the jobs to the real owners of the country." With this tactic, the leaders' aims were to make their nations hate these minorities or at least to make them moderate racists. They were successful. This was the case in both the Armenian and Jewish genocides. During those times, both Germany and Turkey were governed by dictatorships and moderate racists obviously did not show any reaction. Nobody tried to stop Hitler when he first invaded Czechoslovakia or when the Ottomans, the ancestors of the Turkish Republic, started to massacre Armenians long before they started their program of complete annihilation. "Moderates," both the ones who lived in these particular countries, and the foreigners who acted as if they were against all this, in fact did nothing at all. In a corner of their minds they approved of everything that was happening. They didn't realize that their silence was encouraging the murderers.

In some parts of the world, racism is normal. Kids are raised as racists. Most members of some nations hate members of other nations because of the society around them. I, the grandson of a man who survived the Turkish genocide against the Armenians, know this very well. Until 1996 my family and I were still living in Turkey. I had a lot of Turkish friends, some of whom didn't know that I was Armenian. Once, I decided to tell one of my friends that I was Armenian. We had known each other for a long time and I was convinced that my origin wouldn't affect our relationship. First he did not believe me. I asked him why he was surprised and how he expected an Armenian would look. "We are just like you," I said. "We don't have horns or antennas on our heads or tails at our backs." He still didn't believe me nor talk to me for a couple of days. I was sure that he had heard false stories about Armenians in history classes, where the Turkish government tries to make citizens hate Armenians. Anyway, later, he came to my house and apologized. We are still good friends now. The fact is that millions of "Turks" back in Turkey do not recognize Armenians and know them only from history books which are full of lies.

I don't think there is a way to eliminate the racist mentality. When we think that we are rid of it, we see it rise again. Unfortunately, hate and jealousy are very important parts of human mentality. Despite the level of civilization we have achieved, some of us can still be the slaves of dark, wrong, unacceptable ideas. However, we must not give up or surrender to racist ideologies and racists. We must teach the young generation to be more tolerant and to love others. We must teach them not to be prejudiced or to discriminate. Maybe this way we can at least eliminate the moderate racists.

Jason Francisco
English 098
Instructor: Sandra Jackson

Educating Minds And Souls

A great number of scholars and thinkers believe that life can be taught in the classroom from books. They believe that what is needed for a person to enter the real world can all be summed up in a few chapters. This has led educators to confine their teachings to the classroom and neglect the possibility that life and experiences could also play a part in molding a successful adult, ready to enter the working world. There are many fields of education where the teachings should include "out of classroom" assignments. By taking their teachings out of the classroom, educators would give their students the opportunity to explore their creative thinking, using experience as a tool. With this thought in mind, we can still find systems of education where the entire syllabus is confined entirely to the classroom. In many institutions, we can still see educators basing their entire teachings on textbooks, with little or no interest in giving their students an all-around education. The subject of business education is of main concern to me, being a business major myself

I feel the theory of business cannot simply be taught from a book. There are many concepts which may seem simple on paper, but are extremely difficult when practiced. Many institutions offer business programs which claim to provide the necessary preparation for a business student to enter the business world. Harvard Business School, which is the cream of the crop, boasts the most number of graduates who have made it successfully in the business world. Their program is based on teaching from texts with no "feel" of the real live world of business. Students learn what they are taught from texts and are expected to put that knowledge into practice. Some of the professors have never even ventured into the business world, and have no business experience. However, they are given the task of educating future business people, just because they possess the necessary qualifications.

"A teacher affects eternity; He can never tell where his influence stops." This phrase is a quote from the *Washington Post,* made by John Altman, a self-made millionaire, and a full-time teacher at Miami University. This belief encourages teachers to teach from their experiences in the business world as well as from textbooks. John Altman believes that "too many business schools focus on an outdated big corporation model, when most twentieth century jobs will be created by small and emerging businesses." This simply means that the syllabus focuses on larger scale business rather than teaching students how to be entrepreneurs. The challenge lies in encouraging students to venture out and take risks, as opposed to only following what they learned in the classroom. By teaching students based on their own experiences, teachers give them a real idea what it is like out there in the business world. Thus, experience is more vital than theoretical knowledge. After all, many of the more successful businessmen in the world do not claim to have a good business education. One such person, William Gates, was even a college dropout, and another, Walter Huizenga, was formerly a garbage man. These people have not had the essential classroom education that Harvard claims to provide in order to be successful. This simply proves that not all business concepts can be taught in a classroom.

The classroom is simply the place to learn theories and concepts. The real education is actually outside the classroom, and it is the responsibility of educators to bring that outside world into the classroom. In the classroom, a lot can be learned, including all the necessary knowledge on how to start and run a business, and how the decisions made affect the business. The classroom is the place where students get the general idea on the problems faced by businesses and how to cope with them. However, the one thing lacking in the classroom is the business environment, where students can have hands-on knowledge of what they have been taught. The most important concept of all, entrepreneurship, cannot be taught in the classroom unless educators relate their experiences to their students.

In short, I am simply trying to say that business schools should bring in "specialists" in the field of business, to give lectures and seminars, instead of just hiring "paper qualified" educators to teach. Being a scholar with the most impressive degrees does not guarantee that one will be successful in the business world. It takes more than that. It takes entrepreneurial spirit to do that, and what better people to teach just that than experienced business people. Entrepreneurship is like a gut feeling that cannot be taught from a textbook. It requires students to actually get involved in day-to-day business transactions which may encourage them to make business decisions and take those risks, and that is what entrepreneurship is all about. There is no possible equation or theory which may explain entrepreneurship. There are no means by which a student may be tested on this or graded. Everyone has his or her own level of entrepreneurship. Although some concepts are too complicated to explain on paper, the theory of business is still necessary as it is the basic understanding of business concepts.

There are, however, some merits to a classroom education. It gives students the opportunity to explore a subject without ever having to leave their seats. It stimulates their minds by expanding their imagination. It makes them think hard and analyze. It does build their minds and increases their ability to evaluate and think logically. Without a classroom education, there will be no creativity in terms of thinking and reasoning. By combining these tools, educators can carry out their responsibilities of helping students develop their minds and souls.

Scholars and educators sometimes fail to understand that it is their responsibility to give an all-around education to their students. They confine their teachings to the classroom, thereby giving their students the bare minimum required to go out into the working world. They fail to see that they can actually influence the lives of people. By not relating their own experiences, or real-life situations, they are depriving their students of the real value of what they are learning. Students should not only be taught how to succeed, but also the consequences and the sacrifices needed to achieve that success. That is what a real education is about. That is why education should not be limited to the classroom. It should be about how to deal with people in the business world, and about how to be ethical as well as ambitious. That is what prepares students for the real world.

Kinney, Terry. "Man Teaches From Experience." *Washington Post* 22 Feb. 1997. *(Section and page # missing).*

Writing is not an amusing occupation.
It is a combination of ditch-digging,
mountain climbing, treadmill and childbirth.
Edna Ferber

Tu Minh Tran--1st Place Persuasive Essay

English 098
Instructor: Lynne Rosenberg

Public Television

For many years, the Public Broadcasting Service (PBS), has served Los Angeles and other communities in the country with the reputation to inform and educate the public. The backbone of PBS is the support from the government, sponsors, and viewers who make their contributions. By this unique way of getting funded, PBS eliminates many negative commercial influences. But like many other broadcasters, PBS requires financial support as its life blood to maintain quality programming. Recently, the life blood of PBS was short-supplied when the government cut its funding for public broadcasting. Is it wise for the government to do so? To answer this question, I think we should look at what PBS has to offer, so we can make a better choice. Your choice of PBS is the choice of intellectual programming, well-intentioned media, and good-value in entertainment.

As taxpayers, we share the common concern: why should our tax dollars be spent on PBS when commercial TV is racing for domination? Commercial TV is free, but "free" here is only superficial; there are hidden costs that we have to pay as potential consumers. The cost is incurred by us whenever we purchase something we see on TV. Usually, a standard half-hour broadcast on commercial TV consists of twenty minutes of programming; the other ten are occupied with commercial breaks. Commercial-based television has introduced a new term, "channel surfing," to the TV culture. This is the result of commercial breaks and people trying to switch between channels to avoid seeing these interruptions. I am among the channel surfers and usually find myself bewildered by an endless fanfare of information. Flipping channels like a pro, I am unable to follow programs completely but only surf program to program. During this time, I cannot avoid being bombarded with ads that lie and ads that are sexually appealing. But sadly, these ads influence viewers into buying products like Calvin Klein jeans and Survival insurance. Even more astoundingly, these ads also target children to buy their products. Some tantalize children with animated magic or special effects to embellish toys which, otherwise, are "good-for-nothing." Thus, in many indirect ways, we also pay for commercial television. On the positive side, our tax money, which pays for PBS, can eliminate these negative influences of TV commercials.

On the programming note, for anyone who likes to see world news, I recommend PBS' *The NewsHour with Jim Lehrer* rather than ABC's *World News Tonight* or NBC's *Tonight's News with Tom Brokaw*. PBS brings value to your time by covering more news and in-depth analysis without biased opinion, while commercial television brings to you journalistic sensationalism, the so-called investigative reports and one-sided commentary. For example,

71

The NewsHour with Jim Lehrer is usually followed by *Round-Table Discussion,* or *Eye-to-Eye Interview* with people who have authority on the issues. ABC's segment of *Your Money, Your Choice* usually attacks the government on its spending. ABC's analysis of the news covers the discussion with its own in-house celebrity experts such as Sam Donaldson and Cokie Roberts. Judging the scope of the news and the extent of coverage, we clearly see that PBS is a much better choice of news for our after-work hours.

Then comes the question of the integrity of investigative reporting. PBS shows the human truth with programs like *POV* and *Rights or Wrongs.* *Rights or Wrongs* exposes human rights violations in the notorious Burma, the war-torn Bosnia, and even the United States. From the investigative perspective, I prefer PBS to commercial TV, for commercial TV tends to capitalize on stories that retain sensationalistic sex and violence. The race for dramas seems never-ending on major commercial networks. More and more times ABC, CBS, and NBC play car testers and safety inspectors. Sensationalism sometimes becomes frivolous. For example, NBC collaborated with John F. Kennedy, Jr. to poll Americans' opinions of an ideal President, who looks like a lunatic. PBS, on the other hand, is more reputable, and its programs are devoted to more legitimate concerns: How can we detect earthquakes? How serious is our water pollution? What is the GNP (Gross National Product)?

Besides news, there are many kinds of programming, ranging from children's programs to educational programs. Retaining their entertainment value, PBS intends to nurture knowledge and curiosity for children in contrast to commercial TV's interest of high-tech selling. On PBS, ideas are inspired with programs like *Newton's Apple.* With the right blend of instrumental music, good humor, and enthusiasm for science, *Newton's Apple* orchestrates an exciting learning experience for children. PBS also caters many of the most popular shows for kids such as *Sesame Street, Mr. Roger's Neighborhood,* and *Bill Nye the Science Guy.* PBS' commercial counterparts, however, have to meet their obligation for higher ratings. Therefore, to get audiences, they invest in programs that are too violent for kids, such as *The X-men* and *Batman-Animated* with little concern for how these programs effect our children. Thus, the nuances of intentions and interests between PBS and others clearly define PBS as a more appropriate host of children's programming.

PBS offers programming that commercial broadcasters do not offer or have little interest in. Unlike its counterparts, PBS educates the public. Nature programming deserves a fair allocation of broadcasting slots. However, commercial TV only sees advertisement fees skyrocket if they show dramas like love-fighting *Melrose Place,* or body-revealing *Bay Watch.* Some nature shows are seen occasionally on commercial TV but only on their special presentations. PBS, on the other hand, has more commitment to such programming. Nature programs are more prevalent on PBS and the contents of these programs change our attitude and, thus, make a difference to our environment. From *Nature,* I am astounded to know that a staggering number of frogs are deformed and scientists suspect that this phenomenon could indicate that our ozone depletion has allowed ultraviolet rays to penetrate the earth, causing seriously harmful effects to these frogs.

PBS shows its counterparts its superiority by re-inventing the broadcasting media into an education media. We can learn many lessons from public television with programs such as *Government in Consent* lecturing on how the government works. From such programs, we can learn how influential Washington lobbyists are and what powers the President has. These programs can be watched for enjoyment, knowledge, or even for college education because many colleges offer in-home classes with materials presented by PBS. Other similar programs are *Psychology Today* and *Geology*. There are many people who think commercial television is entertaining and public television is not. Apparently, these are the people who perceive entertainment as sex and violence. Programs on commercial TV are getting more "sleazy" and more violent. The madness for sizzling dramas like *BayWatch* causes *Melrose Place*, *Relativity* and many others to sprout like mushrooms. *The X-Files* gives birth to *Millennium*; both are weekend thrillers that give audience double doses of haunted horror. Unlike what commercial TV endorses, entertainment can be in many forms: arts, music, comedy and even science. Besides educating the public with earnestness, PBS also entertains. There are many comedies, operas, and concerts from classical to modern music, like the John Tesh concert. *Mystery* is a two-hour drama of crime investigation. The crimes are conspicuous and none of them are depicted in violence on PBS.

In short, I think PBS offers much better taste than commercial television because it is an apparatus driven by our desire to explore, to conquer, and to know; commercial TV is a multi-billion dollar business which is driven by the relentless force of commercialism. Thus, rather than relying on commercial TV as the only source for our information and entertainment, we should support PBS financially and also politically, by writing to Congress not to pass laws reducing its funding for PBS.

Michelle Silver
English 098
Instructor: Marlene Pearson

Don't Shut My Door

Andrew Lam's essay, "They Shut My Grandmother's Door," reveals much about the way American society views death, as well as the comparative views on death in other societies. The author explains his experiences when dealing with the death of a family member, friend, or a mere stranger. He explains that in his hometown in Vietnam, death is viewed quite differently and taken more seriously than it is in America: "Though the fear of death and dying is a universal one, the Vietnamese did not hide from it. Instead we dealt in its tragedy. Death pervaded our poems, novels, fairy tales, and songs." The author further explains that in America death is not treated with respect and dignity, like in Vietnam: "But if agony and pain are part of Vietnamese culture, pleasure is at the center of America's culture. While Vietnamese holidays are based on death anniversaries, birthdays are celebrated here. American popular culture translates death with something like nauseating humor. People laugh and scream at blood and guts movies." Sometimes it is hard to believe how differently our American society views death, as opposed to another society, like Vietnam. I often wonder how two societies can be so different from one another.

Lam explains that in Vietnam, when one dies, one dies in the comfort of one's own home, surrounded by neighbors, and family, who then mourn the death. He explains that in Vietnam, no one is scared of death, or is fixated upon it, so that when it comes, no one "shuts your door."

In America, most elderly people spend the last years of their lives in nursing homes, where no one cares about them as individuals, and where they are rarely surrounded by neighbors and family, if any at all. When someone dies in a nursing home, the attendants close the deceased patient's door, so that the rest of the world that still lives can be foolishly blinded to reality. Once the doors are shut, it is most uncomfortable for one to pay respect to the deceased, and offer a final farewell. Why do these societies' values differ?

Living in a world where moral values were once considered wholesome and practical, but are now unfortunately considered archaic, it is easy to see why our value systems have gone down the drain and swallowed our moral and ethical belief systems too. It is unfortunate that we live in a world where violence has become an ordinary part of our lives. One no longer is surprised, when listening to the news, by acts of violence. Americans no longer grimace, or turn away, when watching a bloody murder scene on television, or at the movies; instead one rather laughs as if it were a comedy show. Why have we desensitized ourselves into believing that death is unreal and can be laughed at hysterically?

Whatever happened to caring for one another, treating the elderly with respect, leading a normal care-free life without any worries about society's influences? Why do we abandon our elderly who were once as vibrant and youthful as any of today's youngsters?

During my eleventh-through-twelfth grade years at high school, I was fortunate enough to be involved in a special program where the youth would visit the elderly weekly to brighten the lives of our lonely elderly. It was through my experiences that I realized that these people had so much to teach me, and that I had many different people's lifetimes to learn about. I listened to stories that could be chapters in our history books. I was given a mere taste of the difficult lives and hardships that they encountered and experienced first hand. It was then that I realized that the most valuable and appreciated gesture that I offered to my friends was my open ear, ready to listen to past stories or just give a shoulder for comfort. I was saddened to find out that the majority of these people's families and friends live far, and therefore seldom visit. Many of my new friends expressed loneliness, and a sense of sadness that they rarely had any visitors. They often told me, "We've been waiting all week long for you to come and visit with us." Although these comments made me feel special and appreciated, I was disappointed in knowing that I was probably the only visitor that they received all week long. I started thinking about their lonely lives that they continue to lead in isolated, cold, dark rooms. I was unable to fathom the idea that my friends sit alone and wait for someone to knock on their door, to let them know that they care, and that they are appreciated.

I don't understand why society neglects our elderly. Whenever I see an elderly person I ask myself, "Was this person always wrinkled and old looking, with work-worn hands, crinkled skin, and a frail frame?" Of course not! When I look at my grandmother, it is no longer painful to see her physical change, but rather I understand that physical beauty is only skin deep and fades with age, whereas inner beauty lasts forever, and never disappears, even with age.

I'm so happy that my grandmother lives with me because, like many elderly people, she has led a difficult but productive life, and now it is time for her to rest in her weakened years. Is it not the responsibility of the children to care for their elderly parents? After all, is it so much to give a trifle back to your parents who have devoted their entire lives to giving you the world? Perhaps, if members of our society look inside themselves and try to put their priorities into the proper perspectives, America might be looking toward a brighter future for all generations to come.

Tamara Demidenko
English 098
Instructor: Anne Kellenberger

Corruption in Health Maintenance Organizations

It is very sad to say that nowadays medicine has become an object of business--it differs a lot from the time when the first doctors cured their patients whether they had money or not. While preparing ourselves to visit a doctor's office, we think about various problems, such as: is the price fair or not, or do they accept the type of insurance that we have? It is almost impossible to find an experienced doctor who is affordable. Also, it is hard to survive and become used to the system where not only the people who cheat the system are corrupt, even mainstream health care is tainted by greed. Our doctors are more concerned about their money than about patients. Insurance companies are drafting biological Life Tables so they can establish "appropriate" rates for their services. But what is the place of the patients in this complicated system? I think that they could be simply described as supplying function. I think that the gap between HMO services and patients' contentment is getting wider and wider.

Usually, good servers of Medicine are residents of beautiful offices where their diplomas from Harvard, Berkeley, or Yale proudly hang on the walls. As for me, when I am sick I do not need the luxury of a doctor's cabinet and a false smile; what I need is warmth, understanding, and, of course, proper treatment. When my family and I came to the United States, the government provided us with Medi-Cal for a short period of time, so we could make our first visits to a doctor. Right after this, we got a lot of invitation cards urging us to visit different clinics. First, we were happy because we felt that people were simply showing care and supporting us, newcomers, in a world that was so weird and unknown at the time.

The first visit impressed my parents and me a lot: a man drove us to the place where the doctors' office was located, and he also helped us to fill out an application with questions about our health condition. Later, a nurse separated me from my parents and placed us in different small rooms where I waited approximately half-an-hour for the arrival of my physician. There it started: the doctor came, introduced herself, gave orders for my analysis, and ran to the next examination room. For a moment I felt that I was somewhere in a factory where all patients are placed on a conveyer. It surprised me a lot when a nurse came with instruments prepared for the blood test. Smiling she said, "Do not be scared, honey, it's not painful at all." I could not think about the unpleasantness of this procedure--my head was occupied with amazement that a doctor who did not talk to me even for five minutes made a conclusion about the importance of various tests. I knew that my health was absolutely normal; slight headaches and drowsiness, which were probably a result of the adaptation to the new environment, bothered me. My expectations were to talk and discuss my problems with an experienced person, but instead I got a false smile and a bunch of tests. As I found out later, my parents had the same procedures. Having bandages on our hands, we left disappointed in American medical structures and dissatisfied with the results of our first visit. Only some time later we discovered distressing news that doctors usually appoint a lot of analysis in order to charge as much money from insurance as possible.

A couple of months later I got sick and asked the same doctor for help since she had all the information about me. I felt weak, and maybe the reason for this was an "under-dose" of vitamins in my organism. After I had described my health condition and shared a possible explanation for this with my doctor, I asked her to review the data of the blood test. She started looking all over the file and admitted that she never got the results from the laboratory; and all this information was presented to me with an innocent face. "Do not worry," she said, "we will repeat the analysis." I was bemused, having no words to protest or argue. I kept thinking, how could this person, who has a title of Doctor, be so irresponsible, or what if I had some serious problem and for all this time nothing had been done to treat it? No doubt, it was my second and last visit to that place.

Some time later, when my Dad got his first job, we were provided an opportunity to select and buy a health insurance policy. I still remember the evening when he proudly presented my Mom and me a thick package of papers describing our premiums, deductibles, and so forth. The real problem was to select the right doctor from the endless list of them (actually it was a whole book describing MD's locations and specializations). Finally, I found a doctor, but this happened in a very unusual way. While waiting for my car to be cleaned, I was reading the same booklet with information about doctors, having no idea whom to choose. Suddenly I heard a question addressed to me, "You must be having trouble with this stuff. Is it the first time that you are dealing with choosing a doctor?" I nodded, and in response to my positive answer, a lady simply gave me the business card of her doctor. "You are going to like him, everybody else does," she said and, apologizing for a short conversation, ran to her car. Fortunately the woman was right; I like my doctor, even though our communication in the main originates through his secretary who is trying to answer all the questions that I have, while the doctor is rushing to satisfy all his patients. However, nothing is perfect in this world. A new "headache" starts right after I get bills from the insurance company. I can spend hours arguing with agents about the incorrectness of the statement.

It would be totally wrong to make a conclusion that all workers of medicine are irresponsible and impersonal with their patients, but I still have a point of view that medical structures are corrupted. Even if the doctor is good and meets all your expectations, you can't stop thinking about the bill that could be surprisingly big. It is shocking that Health Maintenance Organizations charge so much money simply for the fact that you passed over the doorstep of their clinic. As a result, many people who cannot afford expensive medical care are practicing self-treatment using products daily advertised by radio and television. Unfortunately this does not work all the time, and even worse, one could have a serious disease that was not cured properly. I understand that medical service is expensive because MD's are paying high rent and equipment costs a lot, and besides, they must have their own insurance. In fact, the price for the education in the cheapest Medical school is around sixty-five thousand dollars, but all these factors should not turn doctors to business persons, and their patients to money bags.

I wish MD's were thinking more often about their Hippocratic Oath and the primary function of doctors to treat with care and understanding, to listen attentively, and to peer into the smallest details. Being a doctor is a huge responsibility because doctors hold peoples' lives in their hands and bear responsibility for them. I am very concerned about the situation mentioned above because my future profession is a Doctor of Medicine. I did not choose it because of the income potential, but because I have a feeling that it is great to help people when they are asking for your help. Also, I want to be sure that my family does not have to worry about Health Insurance and bills.

At the conclusion of my essay, I would like to make a proclamation to everyone who is going to devote himself or herself to Medicine: Please, do not think about the profession of a Doctor only as a source of profit, think about it as hard emotional work that requires the maximum of your attention.

Creative
Section

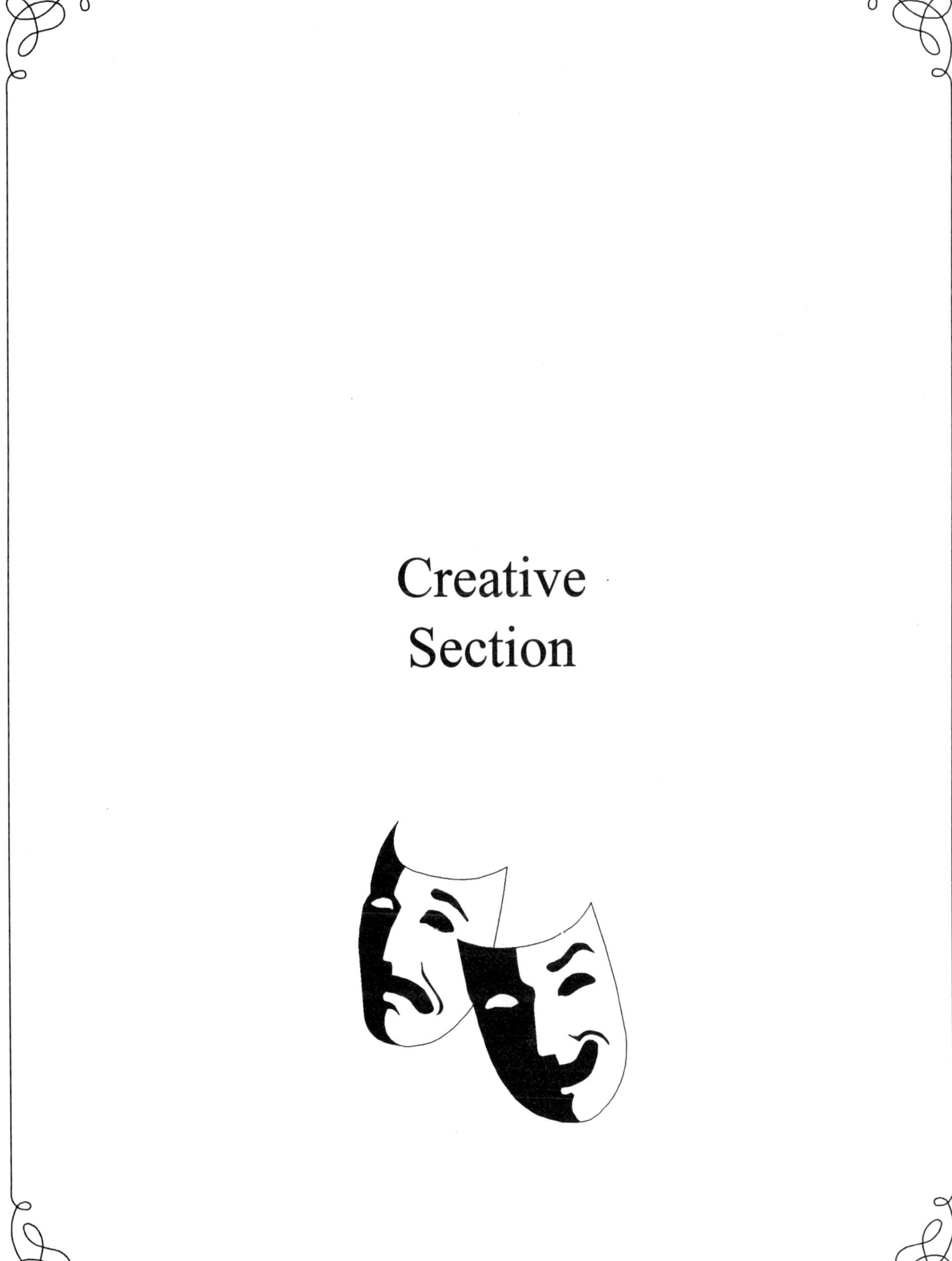

Francisco R. Salas
English 098
Instructor: Debbie Bogard

Santiago

From my great-grandmother's garden I could see the land the people called Santiago. The scenery was breathtaking. The bell-tower on the church peeked over the hills making sure everyone was able to see it. To the far right, crystal-clear water bled from the tall vegetated mountain. To the far left, dark green fields of corn covered the land and made distant the rest of the world as the Atlantic made America distant from Europe. Five-foot tall rock walls that separated the land held the different colored lands together. A river named "El Rio del Sauze" flowed slowly behind the church; it originated from the tall mountain at the far right. From where I was, hanging over my great-grandmother's wall and dangling my feet above the ground, I could see women and children the size of ants, washing their clothes and swimming in the river.

Dinggg...dongggg...dinggg...donggg...A loud sound ran through the valley and finally up the hill to where I was. It was the church bell which rang everyday at twelve o'clock. I should have noticed the time when I smelled the handmade maize tortillas and the steamed beans, which by now were boiling in the ceramic pot. Patience and time put into these foods reflected in the mouth-watering flavor.

That was going to be the last time I would hear the bell that summer. My mother and I said our farewells and we were on our way back to America. As we drove over the rock-covered roads and through Santiago, we were accompanied every step of the way by the smiles, waves, and good-luck wishes of the people. These were the last images in my mind of Santiago, the land of my roots.

Marjan Mansourian
English 097
Instructor: Colleen Schaeffer

Yellow Flower

It smiled at me,
So lovely and beautiful,
Divinely beautiful,
Shining like pure diamond,
In the beaming sun.
Its petals,
Each looked as delicious as a ripe banana,
One wrapped carefully around the other,
All dancing with the day breeze,
Yet flirting with the rays of sun.
A drop of transparent morning dew,
Nestled between two petals,
Magnifying the beauty around,
Taken by the glory.
The dew trembled down the silky petals,
Dropped on a leaf and fell to the ground.
One little yellow rose,
In the mist of such heat and smog,
Brought so much joy and energy to the passer-by.
Oh, what an appealing moment it was!

Jay-jay Loteria
English 098
Instructor: Sandra Jackson

Cover Letter #1

Dear Reader,

Freewrites, focused freewrites, brainstorming, and clustering. These are just a few writing processes that I have learned over the past months in my English 098 class. These methods of writing allowed me to get ideas on what to write and how to organize my ideas. Before, my writing style was unclear and unorganized. Over the few months in this class, I have seen a dramatic change in my writing skills.

Before coming into class and not learning the different methods of organizing a paper, my essays were below average, as I learned coming out of high school (even my high school teacher in AP English didn't think I could write). Now that I have learned these methods, I am able to write well-written essays that have "grabby" introductions, a body with enough information on things that I write about, and summaries or conclusions that go well with my introductions. As far as revision is concerned, I did not know the difference between revising and editing. Now that I have understood what the difference is, the revisions on my papers are thorough and in place. My editing has improved, from putting a necessary comma when it's needed, to placing the proper quotation within a sentence.

From all the papers that I have written in these past few months, I have to say that the best paper that I have written would be the argument paper, "Dress For Success." Although I put more feelings in writing my personal experience essay, "Short-lived Fame," the argument paper allowed me to experience the research process of writing. In turn, I developed an essay filled with information on why the school districts should implement school uniforms. I chose the topic on dress codes because I know, from experience, that uniforms create a safe learning environment and also make a sort of equality between the rich and the poor. The first draft of this essay was good, although there were some awkward sentences that did not make sense. I realized this from my teacher, who, in her comments, wrote that the sentence was awkward and unclear. This is one problem that I have in writing. Often I know what I am writing but I cannot put it into written words as well as I can by telling. The revision of the paper took a little time from my work since the idea of dress codes is a topic that I have knowledge of. The hard part, however, was putting my own ideas and opinions with those of the factual information.

All in all, I believe I have reached a level of maturity in writing my essays. I have developed a skill that I can use in many years to come here at California State University Northridge (CSUN). There is, however, a flaw in some of my writing that I still have to improve on. I need to write more clear sentences and learn consistent usage of past and present tenses. In contrast to this weakness, my strength in writing a paper is how orderly I put the facts and opinions. Also, my introductions have often caught the readers' attention and by doing so they are then seduced to read further on.
Sincerely,
Jay-jay Loteria

Richard H. Min
English 098
Instructor: Sharon Maselli

Cover Letter #2

May 9,1997

Dear Inspectors,

Good morning!

My name is Richard H. Min and I am a constructionist who is in charge of building an English Department building at California State University, Northridge. I would like to tell you about the history of the construction of this building. Since February of 1990, I started to contruct the foundation of the building, and I spent almost 6 years trying to finish this job. The reason for spending a lot of time on the foundation is because I believe that the foundation of any structure is the most important step of constructing and this is my philosophy for strong construction. The foundation has to be solid and strong enough for the pillars and the roof to be stable. During the period of construction, I learned about all the basic requirements for what this building should look like, and I am proud of what I have done so far.

On November of 1996, the construction of the first pillar was finished successfully with the help of an instructor who taught me how to build a strong pillar. I was very thankful for what she had done for me. Recently, I just finished constructing a second pillar of the building, and now, it is the time for you to inspect the second pillar. And I look forward to hearing your comments and advice on the construction of the second pillar. If you think the construction of the second pillar is weak and not solid enough to hold the roof, then I will be glad to rebuild it again. However, I believe that the construction of the second pillar is as successful as the first pillar, and I would like to start building the third pillar of the building. I hope you will agree with me! Thank you for your valuable time!

Sincerely Yours,
Richard H. Min

Writing is a question of finding a certain rhythm.
I compare it to the rhythms of jazz.
Francoise Sagan

Denisha Mathis

English 098
Instructor: Sharon Maselli

Cover Letter #3

Dear Reader,

Open your mind, grab a coke, and sit back. Prepare to be enlightened by the narrative and persuasive tales, as told by Denisha Mathis, a new and upcoming African American female writer.

English 098 helped me to paint a clearer picture for the reader. Throughout the course, I became a more detailed writer, which helped capture the reader's attention. My writing went from "Amusing!" to "Oh...how exciting!" As my writing improved, the readers began to identify with my pain and sorrow. My pain began in the narrative essay, "Grandma Dearest." "Grandma Dearest" was painful, but I enjoyed writing it. The essay is about my growing up and taking on responsibilities that I was too young to handle. In the persuasive essay "What's In A Name?" I did not have pain or joy. Although I enjoy arguing topics such as stereotypes, I did not enjoy writing this paper because I would have gone on and on about how I feel about the topic. My joy begins in the text-based essay, "The Bean Trees." It makes me happy to see people help others who are less fortunate.

As a writer, I try to focus on issues that appeal to the reader. I believe this is my strength. I need to improve on my transitions in writing. English 098 has been an eye opener; this course has set the foundation needed to succeed in English 155.

Denisha Mathis

Rima Ballout--Special Creative Award

English 097
Instructor: Margie Crawford

The Godfather

Finally, after several months of a long and hard wait, Alice Hoffman's new baby is being delivered: *Turtle Moon*, a novel that was brought to light following long months of dedication and inspiration.

Alice Hoffman was very much excited. Millions of thoughts were wandering in her mind. How was this baby? How would it be welcomed in this new world?

From day one, I asked Alice her consent to be the Godfather: her silence was the approval. Since that day on, I was there--days with my thoughts, and evening in person, watching over her work and my new baby. "PATIENCE IS A VIRTUE."

"Every May, when the sea turtles begin their migration across West Main Street, mistaking the glow of streetlight for the moon, people go a little bit crazy" (3). When that happened, as it always did, I gave them my free advice as crystal thoughts and a light mind...HOPE.

I told them to be patient; walk like a turtle, slowly but with a definite goal. At the end the turtle arrives, and so, will you too, with patience. Walk, think, and forget the month of May and how it drives people crazy. Forget the actions and how it made people avoid making any major decisions. How they want to quit their jobs, smack their children, or run off to North Carolina with the serviceman who just fixed their VCR.

Walk and pass the month of May. I'll be with you, helping you, and holding your hand. I am your friend. I will always be here, waiting for you to call on me. Look into my eyes and you will see a smile on my face. I am always there in good times and in bad times. I still remember that day when Lucy's parents died: "If only there had been a full moon" (259). I heard about the death of "Scott" and "Paula" who were killed at a Long Island Railroad, on the way home from a June wedding in Bellmore. They were found with their arms wrapped around each other. I ran too fast, but I forgot an important thing to take with me: Life itself.

If it was a full moon. If..., and if..., a word I hear all the time, but it will never bring the dead to life. The time ran too fast and all of a sudden, I was there taking the life from Lucy's parents to give it back to Julian and Keith: "And a white moon rises to remind them that they are both still alive." Really it is a small world. This time I was there but I didn't get dressed in my funeral suit, I got dressed in my favorite one: my white suit. The white color brings with it hope, security, and peace.

In this world, nothing is free. Remember that to get happiness, someone has to pay for it, no matter what or who you are, a person or an animal, like the dog Arrow who sacrificed his life for his best friend Keith.

I know that it will hurt but we have to look at the positive side that we are still alive. We appreciate what was done but life has to go on, and optimism is what gives hope. I know it's not easy missing someone you love, but this is not the end, life keeps on going. It is like a theater and we are the artists. Everyone of us has a role that will be continued by his or her successor.

I didn't say that because a dog died, or because animals are worth less than humans; as Julian said, "They've never looked into a dog's eyes. They've never stood beside a dog when the moon rises and fills up the night." Just because Arrow never talked did not mean Arrow didn't have feelings. His eyes talked instead of his tongue and if you understand your friend you can share his feelings without saying any words, as Keith and Julian did. They both knew the needs of their dogs and became their friends and they dealt with them.

If you looked into Arrow's eyes you could feel the power of his feelings because the eyes are the mirror of the heart, and when you understand the eye language you arrive at the heart, and the shadow becomes a reality and the darkness becomes the light. The death of Keith's dog was painful. The only thing he truly wanted was his dog back. This, in addition to the thought that he would be with his mother in the same car on the way to the airport, kept Keith awake that morning long before dawn, when there was still a moon in the sky (277).

I know the feeling of regret, especially when you've done a wrong thing to someone who really cares about you. Finally you will ask yourself, "What did I do and why did I do it?" You'll be sad, angry at yourself, trying to forget what you have done; but you cannot. It is your conscience. Don't worry Keith, I know that you have changed. You grew up and I'll be always there guiding you and helping you to move forward. Even you know deep down that you have changed for the best, and all this because of the hope, because of me. Do not ask me why. I just knew it. Maybe because I was always there, following you every step of the way, and sharing with you every aspect of your life.

I am your Godfather: I am the moon.

Now you are safe; you can continue on your life by yourself because there has been a full moon.

With all my love.
Sincerely,
The Moon

**Nadine T. Coury, Sophia Duan,
Tina Duan, Johnny Hodgson,
Vicky Moraza, Larry Stephen**
English 098DF
Instructor: Evelyn McClave

Letter to the Author of *Farewell to Manzanar*

May 8, 1997

Ms. Jeanne Wakatsuki Houston
Santa Cruz,
CA 95062

Dear Ms. Houston:

We are students at California State University, Northridge. We read your book *Farewell to Manzanar* in our English class this semester. We enjoyed reading the book. When we read through your book, we became fascinated with your story. We discussed issues like cultural conflict, ethics, and bad experiences with bad people.   We wrote essays about the story.

We are seven Deaf students of different backgrounds and have barriers in our own lives. Our cultures are American, Mexican, Chinese, African, Trinidadian, and Lebanese. We are also part of Deaf culture. We do not discriminate against each other, because we respect each other. We treat each other fairly. We face discrimination every day in our lives.   It is a challenge to overcome it, but you and your family never gave up. We, too, keep on trying no matter what happens.

Deaf people have no opportunity to become president in hearing high schools. Some special education teachers don't encourage Deaf students to challenge hearing people. Family and friends encourage us. Deaf people have to work harder than hearing people to be able to accomplish what they want.

In sports, at first, hearing people avoid us. It is hard for the Deaf to be on a hearing team. The coach doesn't want to waste time communicating with us, and most of the coaches don't know how to sign.

It's difficult to get the job we want to get. It's rare to see Deaf people who have executive positions at their jobs, or people who are CEO's for their companies.

Your book reminds us about what happened to the Japanese people in America. It will help us to fight whatever happens to us. Your story really inspired us.

Sincerely,

Nadine T. Coury, Tina Duan, Vicky Moraza,
Sophia Duan, Johnny Hodgson, and Larry Stephen

Colleen Devlin--Special Creative Award
English 098
Instructor: Kathleen Boylan

The Mission of a Lifetime

At exactly 9:15 this morning, my captain called me into his office for an extremely important meeting. As I followed behind him, he seemed quite distressed and overly nervous.

"Detective Sanders," he began, "I have an odd mission that you must successfully complete. There is a fugitive running loose in the streets of Los Angeles."

"Yes, Captain. There are probably quite a few of them out there with the way the world has gone down the tubes," I joked.

"This is serious Ben," the captain snapped. "There is a woman, Felice Cumpleano, who has come from the year 2050. Somehow, she traveled back in time and has ended up here. I don't know why she picked this time, but the only thing I do know is that you have a very short time in which to find her before she alters the future, and this makes her dangerous."

The captain handed me a picture and said, "This is what she looks like, and other than that, all you have is her name. Good luck and don't fail. The future lies in your hands." Walking out of his office, I glanced at the picture. To my surprise, I recognized the woman. I had seen her at the local cafe about five days ago. She seemed to look like any other business woman wearing the typical navy-blue pleated slacks, a white silk blouse, and navy-colored low pumps. Her bright red hair, her fluorescent pink nails, her anxious behavior, and the fact that she sat at a cafe table with no food to eat made me take notice and remember her.

"How am I ever going to find this woman?" I thought to myself. "She could be anywhere in this city by now."

At 11:00 a.m., I arrived at the little cafe to search and see if there was anything I could go on. It was just as hot in there as it was when I had seen her. The air conditioning evidently was broken and the heat from the kitchen was bellowing into the dining area. I could smell the grease and fat frying, and I could hear the yelling of the waitress' orders to the chef.

I questioned some of the customers, asking if they had seen the woman in the photo. All denied recognizing her, except one man. He claimed to have seen her alone in the cafe a couple of times this week.

"I saw her crossing the street to that motel just a minute ago," he said as he pointed out the window.

Excited that I was "hot on her trail," I quickly thanked the man and ran across the street to the motel to inspect. It was not the best of places. The building was a dull yellow color and there were mouse traps scattered throughout the lobby. There was also a foul stench in the air similar to the smell of milk that had been left out of the refrigerator for a week.

I asked the manager for the motel register. Looking carefully through the list, I found that room 214 was rented under the name Felice Cumpleano. Excited at how well my search was going, I told the manager to take me to the room.

The room was in the back of the second level of the motel. The manager opened the door for me, and then quickly left I stepped cautiously, with my gun drawn, into the room. It was completely a mess. Looking around, I observed that the bed was unmade, all the lights and TV were on, and the trash can was turned upside down. I went over and picked it up, and there, on the floor, was a piece of crumpled-up paper with scattered stripes of fluorescent pink nail polish. My heart was now pounding, as I thought that I was finally getting somewhere. I unfolded the paper and on it was an address: 1525 Maple Street, Brentwood.

At 2:00 p.m. sharp, I ran to my car and started to drive to the address. As I was driving, I had thousands of questions running through my mind. Who is this woman? Why is she here? Why was I chosen for this mission? How come everything is going so quickly? And why is this mission so easy? My thoughts were interrupted as I turned onto the street. It was a residential district in the rich area of Brentwood. All the houses had a BMW, a Porsche, and a Mustang parked in the driveway. Every house on the block had two-stories and two separate wings. There was even an intercom system at the gate of most houses.

I found the house marked with the number 1525 and drove up its driveway. It didn't seem out of the ordinary. It was just as large as the other houses and it had a New Mexico style of architecture with an adobe type roof and cactuses throughout the front yard. The only strange thing I did notice was the large number of cars parked near the house.

I got out of my car and walked timidly up to the front porch. It seemed extremely quiet inside when I peered through the windows. As I went to knock on the front door, I noticed it was ajar. I pushed it open slowly and called, "Hello. I'm Detective Sanders. Is anyone here?"

"Surprise!" yelled a crowd of people.

Shocked-scared, I stood motionless in the doorway. I quickly looked around the entryway of the house and took notice of the people there: my wife, my captain, my fellow detectives, some friends of mine, and Felice Cumpleano smiling at me.

"Happy Birthday! It took you long enough to finish your mission," my captain teased.

"What?" I asked quite puzzled.

"I set up this mission about a futuristic criminal and faked the clues to get you here for your surprise birthday party. I even hired a woman to play the part," he explained between laughs.

"Did you forget that it was your birthday?" my wife questioned.

"Of course not! I knew what was going on all along," I lied, trying to cover up my embarrassment.

Biographies

Geobert Abboud: First of all, I love writing (especially poetry). I took a creative writing course in high school and enjoyed it quite a bit. From then on, my way of writing started improving. I learned how to write poetry, non-fiction, movie scripts, and research papers. So, I can very well say that I do have a good background in writing. I hate speaking of my emotions, but I love to express them in my writing through fictional characters and, of course, in my poetry. I'm only seventeen and have a lot more to learn about writing. I've started with one of the most basic courses, 098, and hope to move on to more challenging classes. Thanks for reading my papers.

Sarkis Aznavour: I was born on April 6, 1978 in Hollywood, California. I am currently a freshman at CSUN and I am planning on changing my major from chemistry to biochemistry. I have two brothers, Michael and Dominick, who are both younger than I am. My parents have taught me to be hard-working and have told me never to give up no matter how hard anything gets. My ethnic background is Armenian and I am a member of the Armenian Student Association at CSUN. So far CSUN has proven to be much better than high school, and I plan on graduating from CSUN. I love German cars, science, and I also like to travel. I have traveled to many countries in the world and it has proven to be very educational.

Rima Ballout: Born on April 9th, 1972, in Lebanon. Graduated from Rimhala High School, and attended three years at the Lebanese University in Beirut majoring in Interior design. Married to a sweet gentleman since 1992. Have 2 lovely girls, Sarah, a 5-year-old, and Reine, a 2-year-old. Presently attending CSUN and majoring in Art. My hobbies are singing, writing, riding bicycles, and enjoying antiques, shopping, shopping, and shopping.

Mary Barmakian: I am 18 years old and am currently enrolled as a freshman as CSUN. I hope to play for the women's soccer team in the fall of '97. I came to college hoping to meet new and interesting people and get a degree in psychology. I come from a family where education has been extremely important since the beginning. I attended a private all-girl-school for high school and loved every minute of it, including the special individual attention I received from the teachers. There was a closeness there that I probably won't feel again throughout my education. My mother has raised me for the last three years of my life and has taught me a lot about life through her liberal ideas about the way things should be. I intended to write this essay portraying a part of my mom's life where she was torn between two loves. However, my space was taken up while trying to describe the characters and I never got to talk of my personal experience of the situation.

Xuan Chung: I was born in Vietnam but raised here in the United States. I was born October 22, 1978. I attended Abraham Lincoln High School and graduated last year. My goals in life are quite simple. I want to become a teacher because I am fond of children. But I am also aware that a teacher has an important job. I want to educate children and help guide them to success.

Colleen Devlin: Born in Burbank, California. Now, she is attending California State University, Northridge and is majoring in deaf studies. She plans to become a teacher for the deaf/hard-of-hearing and also work as an interpreter. She enjoys collecting Star Wars' action figures and writing personal essays with ironic foreshadowing. However, her favorite pastime is going to Disneyland to recreate a "childlike" atmosphere.

Jason Francisco: I'm 23 years old. I come from a military family where my father and grandfather were both officers in the Army and Marines, respectively. I spent my teenage years in Dunthren Military Academy. I then spent 5 years in the Army, and rose to the rank of Lieutenant. I have a degree in Military Science and spent the most part of my military career traveling from one base to another, throughout the world. My experiences have made me a reservoir of information, bound by flesh, waiting to be put to paper. Writing has always been an outlet for me...a way to express all my feelings. In a way, it is therapeutic, a way to get over pain and to appreciate joy. To me, writing has always been a battle to keep my sanity...and my pen is my weapon of choice.

Emilda Generalao: My nickname is Emy and I am 18 years old. I have lived in the state of California my whole life. I also can truly say that I am a valley girl…"Like, really!" The only out-of-state places that I have been to are Hawaii and Nevada. My true love is acting, though I have majored in Finance. This way, if I don't become rich and famous, I could still be rich with a degree in Finance. Hey, you've got to have a fall-back in everything.

Jay-jay Loteria: Coming from the Philippines in 1991, I spent most of my teen life here in Los Angeles. I learned a new lifestyle, going through the years promising myself that I will make my mark here as I did back in my country. I went to junior high school at John Burroughs Junior High from eighth grade to ninth grade, skipping seventh grade. From there I went to Los Angeles High School where I graduated in 1996. In junior high I took honors classes that challenged me to handle high school academics. I proved to myself and to others that I can handle such education. In high school I became a magnet student in the College Incentive Program and Math and Science Program. I graduated with honors. Now I am currently a freshman here at California State University Northridge (CSUN). I again would like to prove that I can handle higher education and will someday graduate with honors.

Marjan Mansourian: I am a 21-year-old Iranian girl. I am an international student. I came to the US to study three years ago. My family is back in Iran. I live here with my sister and my brother. My major is dietetics and I would like to be a registered dietitian in the future.

Richard H. Min: I am a freshman at California State University, Northridge. I am majoring in Computer Science which is the most popular major at CSUN. Perhaps it is the second most popular after Business. I have a younger brother and since my mother has only two sons and no daughters, she always admires her friends who have daughters. Therefore, I have to pretend to be like a daughter to my mother, so I talk to her about almost everything and even the things that sons don't normally talk to mothers about. I really enjoy our conversations and am glad that my mother is my mother.

Sergio Miramontes: I was born in Mexico City in 1978. I came to the United States when I was seven years old and have lived in the San Fernando Valley since. Currently I am a freshman at CSUN. Through that time of education I have developed interests in many different areas such as music, computers, business, politics, economics, and literature. When I am not engaged in one of these, I work on my education.

Thuc Duy Phan: I am Vietnamese. I was born in Hue, Vietnam. I came to the U. S. in 1990. My major is Biochemistry. I am a Buddhist. I have stayed in a monastery for one year.

Javier Pina: I am presently a freshman majoring in the field of Child Development, and I am the first in my family to attend college. I am the oldest of five siblings and hope to be a role model to them so they can continue on to higher education. I love my family, hot rods (1932 Ford sedan), artistic talent (the DOORS), and my girlfriend (Elvira). I also had the opportunity to have Sandra Jackson as a professor who helped me out when I was struggling with grammatical errors. Thanks Teach!

Christian Popescu: I am a 22 year old freshman at CSUN majoring in Marketing. I am a foreign student from Germany. But as my name might tell you, my origin is not German. My father is Romanian and my mother is Turkish. They migrated to Germany in 1973 to offer me a better future in a more advanced and civilized environment.

Cristina Rosales: I am currently a Freshman enrolled in English 098 with Professor Eve Caram. My major is Business Management and I plan to pursue a career in Human Resources and minor in Speech Communication. It has been a good semester for me, especially because I have learned more ways to improve my writing skills. At first I was hesitant to write, but because of English 098, I am now prepared to write essays for my other classes.

Michelle Silver: Hi, I am a freshman here at CSUN, and so far I am an undeclared major. I really don't know what my career goals are but hopefully I will find them here by learning about all of the vast choices that are in front of me. Right now I'm leaning towards a career in broadcasting or law. I know that the tools that I have learned to use in 098 will enable me to fulfill another dream of mine--to write novels. I have always felt that writing allows one to unlock the doors of the imagination. There is a child in all of us, just waiting to be extricated by our imagination. Let it run, you never know where it will end up.

Jason Spadaro: Born in Panorama City, California on December 1,1977. He is a native of California who presently resides in Moorpark which has been his home for the last 19 years. He attended public school there and received his High School diploma from Moorpark High School in June of 1996. After being accepted to California State University Northridge, he decided to further his education there where he is now a student. In his first semester at CSUN Jason was enrolled in a developmental writing class where he has written various essays. When not in school, he works part-time and is active in his church youth group.

Yuria Takehana: I came to America from Japan one year ago. I missed home at first, but then I realized that what I missed was my past. I love my childhood memory too much to face the reality in front of me. People I loved have passed away, and the places I loved have been changed. I came to America to run away from the reality.

Tu Minh Tran: I was born in Saigon, Vietnam and migrated to the United States in 1988 when I was fifteen years old. I started to learn the English language with what I had carried with me from Vietnam--a knowledge base of the English grammar. Even though I was studious in Vietnam I had a lot of trouble in English and I learned a lot when I came here to the United States. Judging my essays with others', I would say my essays need to be better structured and have a better choice of words. "English is everything"--that's what my teacher in high school once said. Well, I don't think it is everything, but it is important whether you major in English or in Computer Science. I am at a junior level, and I always regret not taking English earlier. Well, there is no need to regret, and I face the English with fortitude and hopefully will succeed in acquiring this important skill. I am currently majoring in Computer Science and hope that someday I will find a job working with computers as I have always wanted. Thanks.